Army Brat

Carolyn Green

Carolyn Green

DEDICATION

To my grandchildren.

Carolyn Green

IT BEGINS

This is the story of my growing-up years as an Army Brat. It covers the World War II years and the years after the war and ends when I graduated from high school.

Not everyone attends ten schools and lives in eight different states and one foreign country in their childhood. Military Brats do. The states may be different and the countries different, but we move around a lot, and that difference is the norm.

I'm proud to be an Army Brat. Proud that my father served our country. Proud that my mother supported him in that service.

Enjoy the story.

Carolyn Green

BROOKLYN

The war finally ended. Daddy came home, but not for long. He elected to stay in the Army. It was a good fit for him. He liked serving his country. Being in the Army fulfilled his purpose in life so he committed his life to it.

He was stationed at Fort Hamilton in Brooklyn, New York. This fort had been around since the Revolutionary War. It guarded the narrows between Brooklyn and Staten Island. Parts of the original fort were still there. I remember running around the walls and gun placement batteries and throwing rocks in the water.

Driving through the gate, there was a large parade ground that centered the fort. The hospital was to the left. Somewhere to the right was Officers' housing, real houses, for a change. We had friends who lived there. The Officers' Club was located adjacent to the old fortifications. For a while, Daddy was in charge of the Officers' Club. That's where I saw my first television set. It was mounted above the bar and usually was playing a ball game, the Dodgers, or the Yankees if they were on. Of course, if I was in the bar that meant that Daddy had taken me to see where he worked, as he always did. And the bartender could be persuaded to fix me a coke if I said please.

Getting to Brooklyn took some doing. When Daddy's leave was up, he left to report to Ft. Hamilton and to find us a place to live, not on post, no housing available, but close by. The movers came to Poplar Bluff and packed up our furniture. Mama and I went to Portia to pick up Aunt Vada. She was going with us to help Mama with the driving. It's a long way from Northeast Arkansas to Brooklyn, New York. I remember spending several nights in motels along the way. Also, since our route took us through some very lonely country, there was a quart jar under the back seat that I used as a bathroom if we couldn't find a place to stop. At least one time we pulled over and headed into the woods beside the road.

But we made it. The furniture arrived, and we moved in. First on the agenda was to see New York City. The three of us headed towards Times Square on the subway. Aunt Vada had planned ahead. She had a piece of chalk that she used to mark the walls of the subway station so we could find our way back at day's end. I don't think we needed it, but better safe than sorry. She took the train back to Arkansas with all sorts of tales to tell.

It was time. I had to start school. First Grade would be at Public School 104. It was close to where we lived because I walked to and from school. Sometimes Mama met me and walked me home. I don't remember much about first grade except learning to read with Dick and Jane, and the time our teacher made us put our heads down on the desk as she came around the room and, looking at our neck hair, predicted what color our hair would be when we grew up. I was currently a cotton top, but she said, rightly, brown hair for me.

At the end of first grade, we had to move. Daddy was transferred to the Port of New York and we had to live closer to his work. We had lived in the second - floor apartment of a typical New York brownstone building on Ovington Avenue. There were also renters on the first floor, and the landlady lived in the basement. Her apartment opened into the back yard, which was not available to the renters. That is why Mama hung our wash out to dry on a clothesline suspended from the kitchen window. The rope was on a pully. She hung up a piece of clothing, then pulled the rope a little way and hung another piece. The whole thing was attached to a pole at the other end of the backyard. I don't know how she handled it if something fell off.

Since the backyard was not available, the kids played on the sidewalks and the stoops. Stoops were the wide concrete steps going up to the front doors. Occasionally, we played in the street, but it was dangerous since cars were parked on the side and blocked other drivers' view.

Our side of the block was all brownstones, and they all looked the same. The other side was lined with real, stand-alone, mostly Victorian, houses. They were mostly residences, but one was a music school. Mama signed me up for piano lessons. Once a week, I had a lesson, and several times a week, I was expected to go over and practice that lesson because we didn't own a piano. I came to hate those lessons. The only thing I can play on the piano is the first three-note piece I learned. "Here we go, Up a row, To a birthday party." I think, but am not lead-pipe- certain, it's C-D-E, C-D-E, C-D-E-D-C-C.

When the kids were playing outside and it was time for dinner, rather than go down all those stairs to the street, Mama would open one of the front windows and blow a horn, loudly. That was my signal to come in. The horn pretty much cleared the block of kids. What also cleared the block on Saturday was Howdy Doody. One of the families down the block bought a TV set, the first one on the block. They were kind enough to let all the kids come watch Howdy Doody on the new-fangled TV set. At my house, we listened to the radio, programs like Abbott and Costello, Fiber Magee and Molly, and The Lone Ranger.

When we moved closer to the port, the neighborhood was a little different. The block was all Victorian houses with front and back yards. We rented the second floor. Well, almost all of it. There was a small room at the front of the house that was rented to a young woman who was a fashion model. We had to share the bathroom with her. She could use the living room and the kitchen downstairs. All I remember about her was how pretty she was.

I spent time in our kitchen, and not because I wanted to. The rule was, clean your plate. Why, because there were children starving in Europe. Why my leaving a few slices of carrot or two bites of meatloaf on my plate was going to help some German kid not starve was beyond me. But that was the rule. Mama and Daddy would clean up the kitchen and leave me sitting at the table until I ate everything or fell asleep with my head resting on the table. To this day, I feel obligated to clean my plate.

I had to change schools when we moved. This time it was P.S. 102. This was the school where we had to square our corners when we walked down the halls, wear cotton stockings held up by kid-sized garter belts, and play on a concrete, fenced-in playground. The same thing might have been true of P.S. 104, but I don't remember.

Something Brooklyn had that I had not experienced before was Catholic Churches. Not that there weren't Catholics in Poplar Bluff. We were Baptists, so they weren't on our radar. My Grandmother Lane (Methodist) did not approve of Catholics. "Carolyn, they worship Mary!" I wonder if she had ever met a Catholic. Probably not. But I knew Catholics. Some of my friends were Catholic. There was a Catholic Church around the corner from our street. I saw them coming and going to

Confession and Mass, the ladies always with their heads covered. One day I witnessed a lady struggling to find her scarf so she could go in the church. It was not to be found in purse or pocket, so she improvised. She took off her gloves and put them side by side on her head and entered the church. No one said Catholics weren't clever.

This time, the backyard was available to us. Mama planted a vegetable garden. No one else in the neighborhood had a garden, not even a few flowers. There was a lot of curiosity about the garden, especially about the okra. You eat this? How? Evidently, Yankees do not do okra. I remember one time mama was so mad at one of the neighbor ladies. She had come to see the garden and asked, when she was told that Mama was from Arkansas, "Do you, and she probably said "youse guys," still live in teepees?" Mama was fit to be tied at that stupid woman.

While we lived on this new street, and it was a numbered street whose numbers I forget, New York suffered a tremendous snowstorm. There was so much snow that the snowplows couldn't keep up. Consequently, the smaller side streets were not plowed. No cars could get through except on the larger, plowed, avenues. Our house was heated by an oil-fired furnace which required a regular delivery of oil. There was no truck coming down our street anytime soon. The oil was getting low and it was seriously cold outside. Somehow, Daddy was able to buy a barrel of oil and get it delivered to the intersection at the end of the block. He pushed and shoved that big barrel through the snow and down the block and into the basement so we could continue to have heat. The neighbors were jealous, and cold.

While we lived in the big city, my parents took advantage of all it had to offer. We visited the Statue of Liberty, even climbed all the way up her arm to the torch, which is 'way up there. We also did the other "way up there" building, the Empire State Building, where you can see to the horizon in all directions. We went to several baseball games in Yankee Stadium. The Yankees were OK, but they never quite measured up to the St. Louis Cardinals, in Daddy's opinion.

At Christmas, we went to see the Rockettes perform at Radio City Music Hall. We attended the Macy's Christmas Parade and I got to sit on Santa's lap inside the store and have my picture taken. We visited all the Art and History Museums and the Hayden Planetarium, where, in the quiet of the stellar presentation, I asked, in a loud voice, "Mama, are we going to get a moon?" The audience laughed. The moon did show up.

We even went up the Hudson River to West Point and to where Rip Van Winkle met his match, and I think there were a few excursions to Staten Island.

Some more traveling we did that I did not like was to get my tonsils taken out. We traveled by ferry out to the

Army hospital at Fort Slocum on Davis Island in Long Island Sound. Why there and not Ft. Hamilton, I have no idea. You go where the Army says you go. Anyway, it was not fun. Even the popsicles they gave me after the operation didn't make it better. They didn't work at home, either. I cried a lot for several days.

But the hospital at Ft. Hamilton did come into play once. I had not been feeling well, wouldn't eat, had no energy, so Mama and Daddy took me to see the doctor at Ft. Hamilton. The doc prodded and poked—took blood— and sent me home. Later that day, there came a knock on the door. It was a nurse and an ambulance sent to take me back to the hospital. There was no explanation as to why they were there. Well, Mama would have none of that. She called Daddy who came and picked us up and took us to the hospital. The blood work had shown that I might have tuberculosis. X-rays were taken, but didn't show anything, so I was free to go. That was scary. Years later, I told my doctor about the incident and he said that there is something that kids get that looks like the onset of TB. Back then, it had not yet been identified, so the doctor was justified in ordering the X-rays.

Soon after, we left Brooklyn. Getting out of the city was good for me. Being in Arkansas was good for me. I have always wondered, but never asked, if Daddy requested a transfer just to get me out of the city environment. Anyway, we were off to Japan.

Army Brat

ME AND MY GRANDMA GONNA' PICK A BALE OF COTTON

There I was, eight years old, fresh out of darkest Brooklyn, a stranger in an alien land. I had come from a place where, against the cold, little girls wore long cotton stockings held up by miniature garter belts, where monitors stood in the school hall to be sure corners were squared, where children recessed in concrete school yards hemmed in by high cyclone fences, and the earth was seldom seen. I had played in the street and on the "stoops" of the brownstones that lined my block. I had watched Howdy Doody on the new-fangled television. I had seen the Empire State Building, the Yankees play ball, and ridden in the subway. I knew quite a few of those Pope-loving, Mary- worshipping Catholics. I had seen, yea, played in, snow. I was familiar with the roar of traffic, the rumble of the El overhead, and the whistle of the cop on the corner.

This was not the same. This was Arkansas. This was the Delta. The Mighty Mississippi River rolled south two counties over to the east. This was the land of lighting bugs and mosquitoes, deep hot dusty roads, broad flat fields white with cotton, and thunder rolling in the night. Here the schoolhouse had four rooms and the school yard was an ancient grove of trees. Here the children played with roly-polies in the dust and cut paper dolls out of old Sears and Roebuck catalogues. People pumped their water from the earth and cooked catfish and hush puppies in a kettle in the back yard. Trains sped through town; they whistled but did not stop. Cows mooed and roosters crowed. Every house had a vegetable garden and a dog, and probably a few cats. The bathroom was 'way out back.

My mother and I had come as sojourners. In six months, we were to join my father in another alien land, his new post in Yokohama, Japan. We were spending the interim with my mother's family; Aunt Vada and Uncle Fred, cousin Tommy, and my Grandmother Lane. When I look back on this time, it seems like time spent in a magic land.

The one draw-back was that I had to go to school. It was summer! You didn't go to school in summer. But in the cotton producing states of the South, you did. So, I trudged off to school, too. Even though I left the second grade in Brooklyn six weeks early, I was promoted to the third grade. In Portia, the third grade was almost complete. The year was winding down when I joined them. In class, reading was no problem. Arithmetic was pretty much a mystery, but then, it still is. The big deal for me was that I was still printing my letters and all the other kids could write in cursive. Oh, the shame! Stupid Carolyn couldn't even write her name. So, the teacher, bless her heart, gave me special attention so I could catch up to the other kids. There really wasn't time before school was out for me to learn much, so my right-handed mother took over the task of teaching left-handed me as we traveled to Japan. By the time I hit the third grade again in Yokohama, I could write cursive, not well, but well enough.

Soon it was time for the school year to end, and King Cotton took over everyday life. There was no doubt that cotton was king, and a very demanding one. In those days cotton was still picked by hand. Every boll was personally pulled by a human hand, and there had to be a lot of hands. In order to supply some of those hands, children went to school during the summer months so they would be free in the Fall to pick cotton, or to support those who did. It was called Cotton Vacation. Ha!

Cotton picking time was an exciting time in the small communities of the South. Everything was different. For one thing, the background noise of life became the constant roar of the cotton gin. Every ear in town was tuned to the sound of the gin and the rumble of the cotton wagons as they lined up to contribute their load of white gold to the maw of the gin. Until the crop was in., life was turned upside down. Little girls took over cooking and childcare and housekeeping chores so their mothers could pick. Or mothers ran the family business so the fathers could pick. Children who were old enough to pick, picked, and no one batted an eye and talked of child labor laws. Families did whatever they had to do to get the best pickers in the fields, for that meant more money coming in.

Money. It flowed out of the fields and into every hand that touched a cotton boll. People had cash to spend. They were momentarily rich. My friends who picked knew that they would be expected to take a large part of their earnings and buy shoes and school clothes, but there was extra money for fun things like ice cream cones and small toys or whatever their hearts desired, just so long as it didn't cost too much. Possibilities abound when you have cash in your pocket.

And now I was to pick cotton, perhaps as much as a bale. I was to have money in my pocket just like my friends. It was arranged. My grandmother and I were to be picked up in the early morning. We packed our lunches, bologna and cheese, a handful of chips wrapped in waxed paper, an apple, a couple of cookies. Water in a pint jar. Our clothes were chosen as carefully as if we were going on an important excursion. First, we each had to have bonnets that not only covered our face but our neck as well. Then we had to have long sleeved shirts and long pants. My grandmother was to wear a pair of Uncle Fred's old pants. I had blue jeans, only they were called dungarees back then. No sandals. I had to wear shoes and socks. Each of us had to have cotton scarves for around our necks. Gloves were debated and decided on, only with the fingers cut out. Where were we going, the North Pole? It was summer. It was HOT. Why did we have to wear all these clothes?

We got up at the crack of dawn, ate our bacon and eggs, donned all our gear, and caught the cotton truck to the field. I rode in the back and my grandmother, because of her advanced age, rode in the cab. Some of my friends from school were there with their families. Everyone knew each other. We gabbed and laughed all the way to the field, though I was more than a little apprehensive about what was ahead.

When we got to the field my agricultural education began. Attached to the side of the huge high-sided wagon that was to hold our cotton was a scale. We would be paid by the pound. Each person was issued a tow sack. It was made of heavy cotton duck, with a strap so we could sling it across our shoulder, and a small tab on the bottom for the hook on the scale to latch on to. Also, it was impossibly long. Longer than I was tall. Actually, my tow sack was one of the shorter ones. My friend Reatha's father's sack must have been eight feet long. When the sacks were full (full?) we were to bring them back to the wagon to have them weighed. The cotton was emptied into the wagon. Then we were expected to go back to the field and fill our sack again. Each person's weight was tallied in the foreman's little book. At the end of the week everyone would be paid in cash.

The foreman gave us his instructions. Choose a row and pick it to the end. No switching. Pick carefully. Get all the cotton out of each boll. Leave the ones that hadn't opened fully yet. Don't throw the unopened bolls at each other. That one was for the kids. My grandmother showed me how to grasp the ripe boll so all the cotton came out in one big clump, and how to shake the sack so the cotton went down to the bottom. We stowed our lunches in the shade of the truck cab. Grandma picked a row and went happily to work, her arms flying to the rhythm of," When We All Get to Heaven." She loved to pick cotton.

For a kid whose only work up to that point had been to set the table and dry a few dishes, I had chosen a strenuous way to begin my career in the work force. First, it was hot, and the day had just gotten started. It would soon go beyond hot to broiling. Second, the bolls were sharp. They reached out and pricked your hand, hard, even causing blood to flow if you grabbed them wrong. Then there were the various and sundry bugs that inhabited the cotton plants. Little red spiders, bigger brown ones, flat armored stink bugs, and wasps. Lots and lots of wasps. I expected to be attacked and stung out of my mind at any minute. That I wasn't was surely the result of my fervent prayer. Flies came to drink our sweat and generally torment us.

Did I have on enough clothes? Was everything buttoned up tight enough so nothing could fly and/or crawl in? Were my pants long enough? Should I tuck them in my socks? Was my bonnet pulled down on my forehead as far as it would go? Now I understood why we were all dressed like Eskimos. Maybe tomorrow I would wear another shirt.

I was pitifully slow. Snails could have passed me like I was standing still. Grandma came and gave me another lesson and a pep talk and I gradually advanced from snail's pace to crawl. The work was hard. All around me the high spirits of the morning gave way to dogged concentration. Just pick, don't talk. Sometimes I moved down the row on my knees, sometimes I stooped. Sometimes the plants were so tall that I had to stand and reach up to pull the fluffy white cotton from its boll. In the first few minutes it dawned on me that, despite my original enthusiasm, I was not going to pick a bale of cotton. If I managed to fill my tow sack, it would be a miracle.

Noon was a welcome relief. We gathered in the shade of the trees that lined the field and opened our lunches. Bologna and cheese were wolfed down like it was prime rib. Even that old hot water from the jar tasted good. The smart ones ate and stretched out in the dirt and slept. Bladders were emptied in the bushes. The young ones talked and laughed until it was time to go back to work. The sacks were shouldered and the afternoon began.

As the afternoon wore on, I picked up the pace from crawl to merely slow. My friends were so much faster I was ashamed of myself. Then my Grandma, with the best of intentions and a great deal of pity, came over to my row and picked with me, putting all the cotton in my sack. After assuring her about a jillion times that I could handle it, she went back to her own row and I trudged on. There's nothing like a little humiliation to spur a person into action.

In the late afternoon missiles begin flying overhead. Hard green cotton bolls whistled by out of nowhere. A head would pop up over a row and return fire. One of the grown-ups yelled at us to stop. The battle lulled, but did not stop. When I got hit in the shoulder, I joined the fray. We had worked too hard and too long and were too bored not to put a little fun in the day.

Maybe the foreman judged the end of the day by the intensity of the battle, for soon the bell rang and it was time to quit. The cotton wagon was left beside the field, for it was still not near full, and we were taken back to town in the pickup truck. The ride was mostly silent, for everyone was dog tired.

Grandma went on home to clean up and get a bite. She said she was too tired to come to supper at Aunt

Vada's house. Never have I been so glad to shed my clothes and get in the tub. In summer, we bathed in the privacy of the smoke house in the backyard. Water was heated in big galvanized tubs set in the sun all day, then it was transferred to a smaller tub for a bath. Mama came and washed my hair and scrubbed my back. She asked about my day and if I wanted to go back tomorrow. Of course I did! Wild horses couldn't have kept me away. This was the most exciting thing I had ever done in my life. It was the only thing I had ever done. I didn't care that it was hot and there were wasps. I didn't care that I got dirty. I loved it! Tired as I was, I couldn't wait for tomorrow.

My grandmother and I picked two more days. I think the family thought I wouldn't last but one day, and that's why my grandmother decided to go with me. But I stuck it out, and she stuck with me. Isn't it amazing and wonderful what grandmothers will do for their grandkids?

By the end of the third day the cotton wagon was full. I had become, not a good cotton picker, but a passable one. I had proudly lugged my tow sack to the wagon and waited with bated breath while it was weighed. It was so exciting to watch when the foreman emptied my cotton into the ever-growing pile on the wagon. Some of that huge pile was mine! Eli Whitney could not have been prouder when the first seedless cotton came out of his gin.

But the absolute best came last. All the children got to ride on top of the wagon on the way to the gin. It seemed like we were on top of the world. As we moved down the road, the wind blew both our hair and the cotton. I think we were there to keep the cotton from blowing out, but our hijinks just scattered it so that every roadside looked like it had snowed. Every time a car passed us, I wanted to stand up and shout, "Look, look at what we did!" Truth was, in the land of cotton, a loaded wagon on the way to the gin wasn't worth a second look. But I didn't care. I really didn't need anyone else to validate my pride.

At the gin, the wagon joined the long line of other wagons waiting their turn to have their white cargo weighed and then sucked up into the maw of the roaring gin. As we reluctantly jumped down from our high perch, I turned my ankle. It was a really bad sprain. The ankle was swollen and purple for many days so that I had to sit around with my foot propped up. Going back to the field was out of the question. Thus ended my agricultural career. I was inconsolable.

I had not picked a bale of cotton, but I had picked some. And I had for the first time earned real money, not allowance money. The foreman came around at the end of the week with my pay. It was, I think, $1.50. Maybe it wasn't that much. What I do remember is that I held on to that money for a long time, finally spending at least a part of my wages in November on the train to Seattle where my mother and I were to catch the boat to Japan.

My eighth year was a year of sharp contrasts. I went from the sidewalks of teeming Brooklyn to the dusty fields of rural Arkansas to the bombed-out buildings of occupied Yokohama, Japan. Since that time, I've grown up, done a lot of interesting and wonderful things, but nothing, absolutely nothing, beats having been a little cotton-picker long ago and far away.

I

ACQUIRING KNOWLEDGE OF LITTLE THINGS

The four rooms of the Portia Elementary School were a far cry from P.S. 102 in Brooklyn, N.Y., but I loved it. This was laid-back education at its best, and I needed some of that in my young life. Living in the big city was stressful. I had been sickly and whiney and generally unhappy. Now I was free of all the accouterments of urban life. Instead, the playground was situated on sandy soil amid a huge grove of pine trees. No more long cotton stockings, no more hats and coats and mittens and closed-toe shoes. The only dress code that I was aware of in Portia was that we had to wear shoes while in the classroom. Not to school nor from school, only while at school. We were pushing the rules a little bit when we took off our shoes at recess, but if we washed our feet off at the pump before we put the hated shoes back on, it was OK. In Portia Elementary School, the rule was, act like decent human beings, be nice to each other, and to say, "Yes, Ma'am" and "No Ma'am" to the teachers.

When I left the second grade in Brooklyn several weeks early, I had been promoted to the third grade. So here I was, a newly minted third grader in the midst of a classroom full of veterans. These kids were finishing up the third grade and I was just starting out. It was July, Cotton Vacation was looming on the horizon and my classmates would soon be promoted to the fourth grade and I would be gone to the other side of the world. In the meantime, I was behind. Oh, I could read with the best of them. That was no problem. Arithmetic was. They had spent the school year memorizing the multiplication tables, and I was just hearing about them. "What do you mean, I have to memorize all of this?" Oh my gosh, what was next? Well, next was the fact that I could not write in cursive. I was still printing my letters. Ah, but geography was a bright spot. I had already lived in the states of Missouri, Mississippi, Virginia, Washington, and New York, while most of the kids in the class had hardly been out of the county. In this subject I was able to pass on my "vast knowledge" of the world. Not that they cared a rat's fanny that I had seen both the Atlantic and Pacific Oceans. Big deal. They were not impressed. The Black River was enough for them. If I began to learn nothing else in that third grade, it was that bragging was not always a good idea, and that it could lead to a serving of humble pie.

The County Public Health nurse had been at school that afternoon, checking us out for whatever diseases might be lurking on our persons. She had checked our heads, our eyes, our ears, and our skin. The note I brought home from school announced that I had head lice and would not be allowed back in the classroom until the condition had been corrected. There was that humble pie!

The smart-ass girl from the big city could get bugs just like everyone else.

You'd have thought I had a raging case of the bubonic plague. The reaction of my female relatives was one of pure horror. I had never heard of head lice, but from their reaction, I knew that this was not a particularly good thing to have. I was about to learn more than I wanted to know about head lice, especially their eradication. Talk about mustering the troops! The Lane ladies, my mother, aunt, and my grandmother, knew just how to attack the enemy. They quickly made a battle plan and sprang into action. Any general worth his salt would have been proud to have them in his army.

My little friends and I were not welcome in the house, so I/we were banished to the back porch, which was a good thing because I loved the back porch. It was really an outdoor room, wide and shady, that ran the full width of the house. It was a haven from the heat in the house and occasionally from the crush of people in the house. The floor boards were gray with age. Over the years, many feet had polished them to a dull grey sheen. At one end of the porch was the swing, long enough for me to stretch out on and read rhythmically, one foot pushing on the floor occasionally to keep the swing barely moving. Accompanying the swing were some old straight-backed chairs and two of those metal lawn chairs that everyone had back then. Aunt Vada's plants resided on a rail that ran across the east end of the porch, geraniums and elephant ears in coffee cans and sweet potato vines stretching from old mayonnaise jars. In the middle of the porch, the back door opened into the kitchen. Attached to the screen door, which slammed with a very satisfying bang, was a large ball of cotton. The belief was that the white color scared the flies away from the door so they would be less likely to come in the house. It stayed there until after the first frost.

On the other end of the porch was the pump. Some houses had the pump in the kitchen, a great convenience, but at Aunt Vada's house it was outside. Built around the pump was a pump stand that served as an outdoor counter. Here vegetables and chickens were cleaned, hair washed, and other duties that required available water preformed. Beside the pump always stood a full bucket of water in case the pump had to be primed. Also, on the back porch was the washing machine, the kind with a wringer. It was pushed back against the wall, swathed in an old cotton blanket. When it was time to wash, it was un-swathed and moved out from the wall, near the pump. While the house didn't have plumbing, it did have electricity. The washing machine was plugged into a cord that dangled from the ceiling. When the wash cycle was through, the clothes were put through the wringer into a large tub on the pump stand, then lugged to the back yard and hung on the line. The dirty wash water was emptied from the end of the porch into the side yard which was always damp and slimy with scum. A large walnut tree shaded that part of the yard and porch, making the possibility of the ground ever drying up unlikely. You dared not run through that part of the yard lest you slip on the slime. If I was in the mood, it was kind of neat, in a disgusting way, to squish my toes in it.

The step up on to the porch was not a real step, just a squared off cypress log from Uncle Fred's sawmill. It was cracked and wobbly and held in place by pipes driven in the ground on either side of it. It still wobbled, but everyone knew it. Had it not wobbled, everyone would have stumbled simply because we all knew about the wobble and expected it.

So, I sat in the swing, awaiting my fate. Meanwhile, the troops were busy. Aunt Vada made a phone call and went off in the car on an urgent errand, and my mother and grandmother tackled the house. The vacuum cleaner ran and ran. Everything that I had come in contact with had to be cleansed. When the vacuum bag was full, it was taken out to the back yard and burned. Then another bag was put in and they started all over again.

Aunt Vada was an accomplished obsessive/compulsive, and her house was her castle. It wasn't much, but it was CLEAN. Every day, the house was scoured like it was Spring. Lampshades, baseboards, chair rungs, all were dusted daily. Floors and counters were scrubbed till holes were worn in them. She wore out more vacuum cleaners that any woman alive. All the little "pretties" she had sitting around had a place, and if they were off by as much as an eighth of an inch they were adjusted back into their proper place. She's the only woman I have ever known who regularly cleaned the top of her refrigerator. And she was short and couldn't see up there. One can only imagine what the presence of lice in her house did to her psyche.

My bed was viewed as something akin to the Black Hole of Calcutta. The pillows were taken out behind the outhouse and beaten, the mattress was vacuumed and turned and vacuumed again. The sheets and mattress pad were born at arm's length to the back yard and the preparations for washing them began. They were obviously too nasty for the washing machine. They were to be boiled. My aunt had a large iron pot, the type in which cannibals always cook their victims in old movies. Water had to be pumped up one bucket at a time and carried to the pot in the back yard. The consensus was that even verminous children can pump, so I stood and pumped a sea of water for the pot. A fire was lit under the pot and lye soap stirred in. The bedclothes would be boiled until the women of the household were convinced that nothing was left alive.

My aunt returned with some noxious brew that smelled like Listerine and my mother sat to work on my head. She sat me up on a stool on the back porch with a towel around my shoulders and parted my hair down the middle. Then she dipped a cotton ball in the smelly stuff the doctor had provided and began scrubbing. She worked from forehead to nape, rubbing as if she was trying to crush the lice with her bare hands. She parted and scrubbed, parted and scrubbed, until my entire head had been treated with the death brew. Then she produced a comb with little bitty teeth and combed every inch of my hair slowly and carefully, all three women examining every strand for any remaining nits. There must not have been too many for I remember their only occasionally finding one. "Is that one, Elsie Jane?" "No, I think that's a piece of cotton." "Well, get it out of there, just to be sure." "See, it was one. Look there, too." When it was all over, I felt the kind of relief that one who has narrowly escaped death must feel. Then, O my Lord!! She did it all over again! Surely, I would be dead before all the lice were!

I must hand it to my mother. I'm sure that her plans for the afternoon did not include de-lousing her daughter, but she never was mad at me for getting head lice. She was mad at me for acting like a brat. "You're killing me! That's too hard! It's in my eyes! It's in my eyes! I need a towel! Quick! Ow! OH! Stop!" I guess I should be grateful she let me live.

As the second treatment was progressing, and the sheets were boiling in the back yard, the women of the family gathered around and the SPECULATION began. It was delicious. I was all ears. Which of the dirty vermin-ridden urchins in the school had given their little darling head lice? Several candidates were discussed, at length and viciously. Those Safels lived like pigs, nasty folk. Who knew who all those kids of Jane's belonged to. Someone had seen a strange car parked in the shadows behind her house on several nights when her husband was working late. Probably that Young boy. He always looked at all the women like he was undressing them. Mayhap he got to at her house. Did you take a look at Reta Lee's hair at the auction on Saturday? Besides being a mess, it was probably alive with lice. Her boy was in the fourth grade, wasn't he? She was rumored to put color on it. It couldn't still be that dark naturally. She never was any good and everyone knew it. Oh, and that little Lawson boy isn't right in the head. That's 'cause his daddy is also most likely his grandpa. If poor Emmy ever had a husband, no one knew about it. Dirty folks, those Lawsons, and on and on until every family considered to be dirty enough to have lice, either in their persons or their private lives, was thoroughly denigrated.

I had never heard people talked about like that. The ladies seemed to enjoy it so much. I guessed it must be fun. Finally, the field was narrowed down to two possibilities. I was instructed to always stay at least ten yards from these hapless children, lest they re-infect me. They undoubtedly lived in indescribable filth and depravity. Back then, nice people just didn't get lice. Lice were something that only appeared among the lower classes. Not the nice, hard-working but just–can't-get-ahead lower class, but the lazy, no-good bum lower class. The possibility that head lice were no respecter of persons never entered their minds. And, by the way, they would rip my tongue out if I ever told anybody that I had ever harbored anything so disgusting as lice.

The second treatment drew to a close. I was still alive, but barely. The sheets were hung, not on the line in the yard, but in the smokehouse. It would be all over town that some of the kids at school had head lice, and sheets appearing on the clothesline when it wasn't wash day would be a sure give-away of a visitation of the nasty bugs. People, if they knew, would say that the Buercklins were dirty. Discretion was called for. It was hoped that no one had noticed the fire under the wash pot nor the goings-on on the back porch after school. Why the ladies thought they could keep it a secret is beyond me. This was a town of maybe five hundred people. There were no secrets, at least not for long. Somebody knew the names of every kid with bugs before we even got home from school, but appearances were kept up.

Amid the damp sheets in the smoke house, I was plopped down in the wash tub to be scrubbed to within an inch of my life. I was just conscious enough to be thankful that they were not boiling me in the big iron pot.

When Mama was finished, I was probably the cleanest I had ever been in my life.

Dinner that night was just leftovers. There had been no time to cook a proper meal. Delousing takes time. Uncle Fred was brought up to speed when he came home from his work at the post office. He already knew about the nurse's visit to the school, but had missed hearing about which kids actually had lice. Or he wasn't told because his niece was one of the buggy ones. He was the only one amused when he found out that I was one of the "Untouchables." He had heard that all the Madison kids had the "itch." That was another group I was to stay away from.

There was some nervous laughter around the table that night. I guess Mama and Aunt Vada and my grandmother thought that all the lice had been gotten rid of and that they had succeeded in keeping my "condition" quiet. It was never mentioned again, except years later, when it was finally funny.

Mama put my hair in pigtails for school the next morning. I had to wear a nice, starched, pretty good pinafore, not the usual beat-up school clothes. All in all, I looked unusually clean, which was the point. No one was to look at Carolyn Jane and wonder if she had head lice. Because of the efforts of my female relatives, my serving of humble pie proved to be rather small, though not a bit tasty.

The thing is, when I got to school, I looked at my classmates and wondered which of them had head lice. Ah, sadly, I had learned to judge the little things.

LEARNING STUFF

Before we went to Japan, my Grandmother Lane wanted me to know first-hand about chickens and eggs. To that end, she took me down the road to her friends' house. "Bless her heart, this child has never seen a chicken house." "Well, we'll take care of that right now." I was ushered through the yard and into the small chicken house. It was dimly lit, with only a forty-watt bulb in the middle of the sloping ceiling. Windowless, the only openings were the human-sized door and a chicken-sized opening at ground level with a wooden "flap" that was secured at night to keep the chickens safe from any intruders with a taste for chicken meat.

The roosts, where the chickens slept, were skinny poles that stair-stepped from ground level almost to the ceiling. Mounted along one wall were the square, shallow nesting boxes, six of them, full of straw, where the hens laid their eggs.

I reached carefully into the empty nest and brought out an egg. "Now get the egg out of her nest, Carolyn. She'll most likely have one." Reaching into an empty nest was one thing; reaching under a real live hen was another matter. Uh-oh! I didn't know about that. Her? That big fluffy bird? What if she pecked me? What if there was something in that nest I didn't want to put my fingers in? Gingerly, I slid my hand under the hen. Sure 'nuff, there was an egg. She was warm and soft and didn't seem to mind that I took her egg, only cluck, clucked a little bit. OK, I could do this. Gathering eggs was pretty neat. From then on, I was sent to gather eggs whenever my grandmother needed them. Eggs that come in a Styrofoam box are easier, but not near as much fun as getting them from the source.

Not only did I learn about where eggs came from, but I also got a lesson in chickens---how they get from the chicken yard to the frying pan. I assumed that the hens were either delivered or Tommy went down to the neighbor's and picked them up. Anyway, there were two hens pecking around in Aunt Vada's back yard. Grandmother Lane carried a large pan to the pump stand and Aunt Vada ran down the hens. She handed one to Grandmother who took it around the neck. Then she lifted the hen above her head and swung. The head came off!! The rest of the chicken ran and flopped around the yard, spraying blood everywhere. Then she did it again!! The other headless chicken also flopped around the yard until she joined her sister in a dead heap on the grass.

I was stunned. And nobody seemed to give any of it a second thought. No one even blinked an eye when she wrung those chicken's necks. Aunt Vada went back in the kitchen promising to come back with hot water. Then Grandmother proceeded to pick the feathers off. Somewhere in the de-feathering process she washed the bodies. When she got most of the feathers off, she twisted up a couple of sheets of an old Arkansas Democrat and set them on fire. Then she picked up each chicken by the legs and singed the remaining pin feathers off. As long as I live, I will always remember the smell of wet, hot feathers. But the process was not finished.

Grandmother then cut up the chickens, discarding the guts and cutting the chickens into recognizable pieces. One of the hens had a fully formed egg in her, which I thought was strangely gross. The pieces were put down in salt water and stashed in the ice box for Sunday dinner. While the whole process was horrifying and shocking, it didn't keep me from enjoying a leg and a wing on Sunday.

Another thing I learned while in Portia was how to ride a bike. I have no idea where it came from. Not many kids in Portia had a bike. It wasn't that kind of town. The bike wasn't new, so it had to have belonged to someone sometime. I just didn't know who or when.

Anyway, I didn't know how to ride it, but Aunt Vada did. And she taught me. We took the bike out to the road and Aunt Vada gave a demonstration, then put me on the bike and ran along behind me, holding the bike until I got my balance. After a few tries and spills, I got it. I could ride a bike!

Then Aunt Vada decreed that it was Mama's turn. Over Mama's protests, she was forced on the bike and the lessons began. It was an exercise in futility. Every time Aunt Vada let go of the bike, Mama wobbled directly for the ditch. After three trips to the ditch, Mama quit. Aunt Vada and I were too weak from laughing to care much. It was painfully clear that Mama was never going to ride a bike.

But now I could and I was free to go wherever I wanted as long as I stayed on this side of town. I couldn't cross the railroad tracks and the highway, but I could go down and gather eggs and I could visit Grandmother and Doctor Buercklin where there was another lesson waiting for me.

The Buercklins were quite a pair. They were my cousin Tommy's grandparents, making me not kin, but family. Grandmother Buercklin was Mrs. Sprat to Doctor Buercklin's Jack. They had six kids, five of whom they raised to adulthood. The good doctor was retired, at least as retired as a doctor in a small town gets to retire. Ethel stayed at home and raised the kids. She always wore a home-made flowered house dress. He kept his pants up with both a belt and suspenders.

They lived on the corner in a big, unpainted house with a long three-bedroom wing connected to the rest of the house by a dog-trot. The big front room had at one time been a general store. Now it was the living room. In this room were their personal chairs, and a big old console radio where they listened to the news and Dr. Buercklin listened to Dizzy Dean broadcast the Cardinals. There were lots of bookcases and plenty of places for the large family to sit when they came to visit, which actually wasn't often. Centered in the dining room was a big round table, an equally big sideboard and a curved-glass display cabinet full of Grandmother Buercklin's collection of miniature vases and pitchers. Sometimes I was given a "tour" of the miniatures, listening raptly as Grandmother Buercklin told stories of where in the wide world they came from and who had sent them to her.

There was a smallish kitchen dominated by a huge wood stove where she baked the best bread I have ever tasted, and a long screened porch out the kitchen door that housed the pump and an assortment of gliders and metal lawn chairs. Out back was a barn, the home of their milk cow and a bunch of feral cats, and an outhouse. There was a poured concrete sidewalk from the back steps to the outhouse, something no one else in town had. But that wasn't the best thing about the outhouse. Inside were the usual three holes—two adult holes and a kid's hole. What was different was that on one hole was a real toilet seat, padded, no less. This was Grandmother Buercklin's seat. No one else was to use it.

Sometimes when I'd go in there, I was tempted to use it, but was too afraid of the consequences if she found out. Maybe I thought I'd look guilty, or she would just know. It wasn't worth the risk. I well-remembered how she had raked Mama over the coals because she had allowed me to get tan. Field hands were tan. Ladies, even young ones, were not tan. They covered up to preserve their pale skin. Heaven forbid that anyone should think that a lady had to work outside in the sun. Mother had dropped the ball. And Mama didn't say a thing! Just, "Yes, Ma'am. I'll get her a hat." (She didn't.)

Ethel Buercklin was not like other grandmothers I knew. She was not a Bible reading, bless your heart, have another cookie type. No, she was the type who took no prisoners. It was Ethel's way or the highway. Dr. Buercklin had long ago learned to say, "Yes, dear." and retreat to the barn or some other safe place.

She was different in other ways, too. For one thing, she was an artist. She painted in oils and water colors, usually landscapes and fair maidens. Her easel was sometimes set up in the dining room and sometimes on the screened porch. Hers was the only art on the walls. And she was a reader. Nothing unusual there. It was what she read that was different. Every adult woman I knew read Ladies Home Journal, Good Housekeeping, Life or Look. Not her; she read magazines on subjects like archeology and astronomy and National Geographic. There was no Bible on her chair-side table. Her hard cover books were thick, serious tomes. Often there was a volume of the encyclopedia on the table with scraps of paper sticking out like she had been taking notes or looking something up. Lots of times when I came, she would be sitting in her chair, feet propped up on a stool. Her legs were always wrapped in ace bandages and she wore large men's house shoes. She would sit me down with a copy of National Geographic and tell me to be quiet, which I did because I loved that magazine.

I also loved Dr. Buercklin. He was a dear, sweet man. It goes without saying that he was possessed of a lot of patience. He was tall and thin, a real Jack Sprat. He had a shock of straight, white hair, longish for the day. His clothes fit him as if he had recently lost weight and had not bothered to get any new ones. The best thing about Dr. Buercklin was that he let me tag around after him. Often, we would sit on the steps of the dogtrot and he would tell me about his rocks. He had lots of them .They were lined up on both sides of the steps, and even spilled out into the yard a little. There was also a sprinkling of arrowheads.

He would turn the rocks over in his big hands, his long fingers caressing them as he told me their names and where they came from and what layer of the earth they occupied and what made them special. Most of it I didn't understand but it didn't matter as long as he was talking to me. The arrowheads were special. Most he had gathered himself along streambeds and from plowed up earth on the farm. He would spin tales of the Indians, how they lived, danced, worshiped, and hunted with these arrowheads that they made themselves out of special rocks. I loved it all. I think he did, too.

Sometimes we went to the barn. I was introduced to his cow and allowed to try my hand at milking, which I never mastered. But he did let me lead her in from the pasture across the road from their house. He would stand on the porch and watch me as I led the cow from the pasture and around the corner to the barn where he met me to milk the cow and put her up.

The cow was not the only occupant of the barn. There was a small pack of barn cats, employed to keep the mice at bay, given milk in an old hubcap, and left on their own otherwise. Mama cat had kittens, four of them. Though I was unaware of it at the time, I suspect that cat birth control took place after the births, the extra kittens either taken out in the country and dumped or drowned in a bucket of water. I was a cat lover and I loved those kittens. As they grew, they would let me pick them up, even though feral mama was not happy about it. Every time I was at the Buercklin's I always went to the barn to play with the kittens.

One day Grandmother Buercklin asked me if I would like a kitten. Of course I would! Would I like to have them all? I was so excited. Four kittens of my very own! Wow!! Grandmother Buercklin smiled a big smile and helped me put them in my bicycle basket so I could take them to Aunt Vada's house. I remember happily pedaling my bike down the sidewalk and up to the back porch at Aunt Vada's. I called everyone out to see what Grandmother Buercklin had given me. The reception was not what I expected. I would not do it justice if I did not describe it thusly: the shit hit the fan. Aunt Vada was more than mad, Mama was madder than I ever saw her in my life and my other grandmother was shocked into speechlessness, which was a good thing since she never missed a chance to add drama to a situation if she could. I could not keep the kittens. I, of course, was devastated and burst into copious tears. The kittens never got out of the basket.

Mama and I marched down to the Buercklin's. I cried all the way down the block. My heart was broken. Never mind that it was explained to me that we were leaving soon and could not take them with us. Never mind that I was promised we would get a cat when we got to Japan. Mama sent me to the barn to unload the cats while she went in to talk to Grandmother Buercklin. I stayed in the barn and was comforted by Dr. Buercklin. He sat on a bucket and held me in his arms and let me cry. I was probably not the only child he was called upon to comfort because of something his wife had done. Soon Mama came to get me and we went back to Aunt Vada's. I don't know what was said, but I'll bet that Mama told her a thing or three about kindness and how she felt about hurting her daughter.

It was years before I knew what really happened. I had been a pawn in the on-going battle between Grandmother Buercklin and her daughter-in-law, my Aunt Vada. Ethel knew that Vada was not a fan of cats. She knew that we were not going to be there much longer. Did she think that she could get away with sticking my aunt with four cats after Mama and I left? Evidently it was worth a try. I guess she thought that they wouldn't break my heart and would let me keep the kittens. Well, she underestimated the Lane ladies. They would not play that game. The cats went back and I was not encouraged to go back to the Buercklin house. I did occasionally go back to see Dr. Buercklin but did not go in the house.

So, what did I learn? That those you think are great can be petty. That it is not right to use other people to gain your own ends. Be careful who you trust. Don't be surprised when mean people do mean things. It is best to be kind. These are lessons everyone learns during their life. I just think it would have been better if I had not learned them so soon.

IT TAKES A VILLAGE

Portia was a little town. There was no doubt about it. Even in its heyday, the most folks it could muster were in the neighborhood of 500 souls. The railroad and the highway divided the town right down the middle. The railroad bed was elevated above the flood plain so when the Black River was out of its banks, the mail could go through. Cars drove up one side of the steep crossing and down the other. That was pretty much it for height. The rest of the countryside was flat as a plate. Oh, and the highway was paved. Nothing else was.

North of town, two or three miles, were the Portia Bottoms, really a swamp. This was probably some of the "sunk land" from the New Madrid earthquake long ago. Inhabiting the stagnant water were cypress trees with their knees breathing in oxygen for their parent trees, Spanish moss draping long arms from the cypress limbs, lots of fish of all kinds, snakes, most probably cottonmouth water moccasins, and, the bottoms most plentiful product, mosquitoes. An uncountable multitude of mosquitoes, big ones, probably the biggest, meanest mosquitoes in Christendom. Until the cold weather came, smart people in Portia didn't go out at night, at least not for long, lest they be eaten alive.

Three general stores anchored "downtown." They were all the same. Each had four large windows and a pair of tall, recessed glass paned front doors. The stone thresholds had a depression worn in them from years of people going in and out. In front of all the store windows were old wooden benches. On these benches is where husbands sat and visited or whittled or napped while their wives shopped or where kids were parked while they ate a drippy ice cream cone on a hot Arkansas day. It was not unusual for the occasional tidbit of gossip to be passed around. In front of the stores ran a concrete sidewalk, cracked and broken, long in need of repair. The three stores shared a tall wooden canopy, designed to keep the sun out, supported by thin iron poles which had all been bent by cars bumping into them.

To the south in the next block were the post office on the corner, where Uncle Fred was the Postmaster, a small "giraffe rock" building that held an insurance office, and a service station complete with garage. Across the road from the station was a cotton gin that backed up to the railroad tracks. To the north were a small café and a few businesses, none of which I really remember except a beauty shop which was around the corner from the last general store. Across the road from the café was yet another cotton gin that backed up to the railroad tracks.

Across the highway from the general stores was the railroad station where the train didn't stop anymore. Uncle Fred took a large heavy canvas mail sack to the station where the station master hung it on a hook so the next passing train could catch it as it sped through town. That was it for downtown. In addition, the town held four churches and an elementary school. The local doctor had his office in his home.

The streets had no names and the houses no numbers. There was no need. If you wanted your mail, you went to the Post Office and picked it up. Everyone knew where everyone else lived. They also knew where you went to church (or didn't), which store you shopped in, if you voted in the last election,--everyone was a Democrat, so party affiliation wasn't a mystery, and how many months elapsed between the wedding and the birth of the first child. They knew where you worked and had a fair idea of how much you made, and an opinion on whether or not you spent it wisely. In other words, there were no secrets.

My friends and I were soon to get a lesson in just how hard it is to keep a secret in a small town. But on this day, we were busy with play. We started the day cutting out paper dolls on Aunt Vada's front porch. We had a much-used stash of her old Sears and Roebuck catalogues and today there was a new one. This was great! There would be new "dolls" with new stances and new clothes to dress them in. We cut out the "dolls" from the catalogue and then cut out clothes for them, adding tabs to hold on the various skirts and pants and blouses and trimming the clothes to fit, sorta. Their arms and legs didn't always go the way the arms and legs of the clothes went. Sometimes an arm went up and a sleeve went down or a leg extended farther that a slim skirt. The paper was floppy so the dolls were floppy, too, making playing with them somewhat of a challenge. But they occupied the morning until Reatha and her sister, another Carolyn, were called home to dinner. In those days, we didn't have lunch; we had dinner at noon and supper at night.

After dinner, I went across the street to my friends' house to see what they wanted to do. It was hot. We read comic books for a while, but were soon bored because we had read them all a jillion times and none of us had money to buy new ones. Reatha suggested that we go down the road to her grandma's house. On the way down there, we stopped for a while to play with the roly-polys. All we had to do was lift a rock or board and there they were, little hard-shelled bugs that were plentiful and fun to play with. We caught some and used our fingers to make tracks for them in the sand. The best, deepest sand was at the side of the road. Passing cars moved the sandy soil from the center of the road to the sides. The roly-poly's curled up in a little ball when we picked them up. We rolled them around in our hands, then dropped them down in the sandy maze and waited until they unrolled and started running down our roads. Then we'd collapse the road on them and wait while they dug themselves out, then do it again. When we got tired of that, we'd play roly-poly marbles for a while. But we soon tired of that, besides, the sand was hot on our feet and legs.

Arriving at Grandma Land's house, we went into the back yard where the hog pen was. In the shade of several walnut trees lived one of the biggest pigs I had ever seen, not that I had seen a lot of pigs. He toddled around on incredibly skinny legs. I didn't see how they ever supported his humungous body. His belly dragged on the ground when he walked. Even his curly pig tail was big. This pig didn't have a name, just Pig. After all, he was destined to grace the Land's dinner table next winter. The object of this trip was to get him to grunt. So, we would grab an old corn cob, get on his back, and set to work rubbing down his mud encrusted sides. Pig had a capacity of two little girls, so one of us hung around on the fence until it was our turn.

The other two of us sat on him and rubbed the corncob across his hairy skin, and he grunted in pleasure, at least that's what we thought. He may have been saying, "Get off my back, little girls, and leave me alone." We took turns and laughed uproariously every time he grunted. We discovered that we could get Pig to grunt in time to our speed with the corncob. Fast, grunt, grunt, grunt, slow, ---- grunt----grunt----grunt. After we each took several turns straddling Pig, he began to lose his charm, and besides, his wiry hair scratched our bare legs, so we abandoned Pig to his own devices. After a quick trip to Grandma Land's kitchen for a drink, and to wash our hands, (Grandma's request) we headed back to Reatha and Carolyn's house.

On the way I told them a joke Uncle Fred had told me the night before. Reatha thought it was funny. Sister Carolyn said, "Who's Prince Albert?" "You know, he's the guy on the red can of tobacco that Grandpa buys." "Oh." She didn't get it. But I knew who would. "Let's call Eldon Watson. He'll think it's funny. But we won't tell him who's calling." Eldon Watson was the proprietor of the first general store in the downtown lineup. He was a big joker. Always had a joke or a funny story to tell. Aunt Vada shopped there so I was in the store several times a week, either with her or picking something up for her. Pulling off a joke on him would be more than great. We couldn't use the phone at Aunt Vada's because she and my mama were there, so we went to the Land's.

Mrs. Land took the little brother and worked at the family service station for a few hours each afternoon. Reatha was the designated caller. She was the oldest and it was her phone. Ring, ring. "Watson's store," said Eldon Watson. In her best grown-up voice, Reatha asked, "Do you have Prince Albert in a can?" Said he, "Well, yes, I do." "Then why don't you let him out?" And she hung up.

We roared with laughter. Then as a body, we raced out of the house and up the road as fast as we could, heading to Watson's Store. Oh, no. no! The train was blocking the road.

Occasionally, trains stopped in Portia. Not to let off or pick up passengers, but to wait until the track ahead was clear of another train so it could proceed on its way. When that happened, both crossings across the tracks were blocked, effectively stopping traffic from moving from one side of town to the other. The wait was usually not too long, a few minutes, but it could be as much as fifteen or twenty minutes. We couldn't wait that long! We had to get to Watson's Store. What were we going to do? This was going to be too much fun to just give up. There was a way, but it was forbidden. Really big forbidden. On pain of death forbidden. We could crawl under the train. Dare we? If we were caught, we would be in big trouble. Every kid in Portia had heard the cautionary tale of the two brothers who were crawling under the train when it suddenly lurched. One lost his leg and the other his life. But we had to get to Watson's store, and quick. To wait until the train moved would ruin the whole thing. We had to get up there while he was still laughing. We would risk it.

We looked around. We could see no one paying any attention to us. In fact, we couldn't see anyone at all. OK, we'd do it. One last look around and we scrambled under the train. It was farther from one side to the other than I thought. And the underside of a train car is scary looking. On the other side, we looked around again. No one was looking. We did it! Off we ran, across the highway and into the store.

Eldon Watson was there. He grinned at us when we burst through the door. I saw a brief question cross his face, but it was gone in a flash. "You girls looking for something?" he queried. Giggles from us. "You sure?" he said. More giggles, and wiggles. "Because if ya'll are looking for Prince Albert, well, I let him out. Didn't know that poor fellow was stuck in that can until I got a phone call telling me he was in there. " We laughed and ran out the door. We plopped on the bench outside and laughed our heads off. When we got our breath, we just sat there enjoying our triumph. Several people coming out of the store looked at us and grinned, so I guess Eldon Watson was telling them what we had done. Pretty soon Eldon came out.

"You girls look like you don't have anything better to do. Miz Jennings needs some things delivered. Why don't ya'll run them down to her house?"

We were each given a half full grocery sack to carry. Mrs. Jennings only lived two blocks away, across from the Methodist Church. As payment, she gave each of us a hug and a kiss on the cheek. When we went back to the store,

Eldon Watson gave each of us a nickel. A nickel! A nickel would buy us an ice cream cone. "Thanks, Eldon!

Watson's Store didn't sell ice cream, but Mr. Garfield's did. His store was the one on the other end of the line. We raced down there and ordered a vanilla cone. There was no choice, he only sold vanilla. Now, sometime in Mr. Garfield's life, he lost his right arm just above the elbow. All his shirts had one long sleeve, the left, and one short sleeve, the right. How does a man with only one arm load ice cream into a cone? Simple. He clamps the empty cone between his stump and his body and dips with his left hand, puts the dipper down and hands you your cone with his left hand. As far as I know, no one ever took exception to his method. We paid for our cones and ate them on the bench outside his store.

The day was winding down. The train had chugged away unnoticed and traffic was moving again. It was time to go home. Each of us had duties to perform to help get supper on the table. We had had a good day, had fun with Pig, played a good joke on Eldon Watson, and gotten an ice cream cone. Best of all, we had gotten away with a high crime and were feeling pretty smug about it. I, for one, couldn't wait to brag about it to our friends, especially the boys who were always calling us sissies. We would see each other tomorrow.

I did notice Mrs. Land standing on their front porch with her arms crossed as we approached the house. Then she went inside. I guessed she was looking for Mr. Land to come home. Good-byes were said, and we went our separate ways.

They were waiting for me when I walked through the door. From the looks on their faces I knew that someone had told on us and I was in big trouble. Mama started, "Carolyn Jane." Not a good sign when she used both names. "Carolyn Jane, you and Reatha and her sister were seen crawling under the train this afternoon. I know you know better. Why on earth would you do such a thing? You know how dangerous it is. You could have been killed." When Mama finished, Aunt Vada started. "Three people called here this afternoon to tell me what you all had done. They saw you all crawl under that train. You do know what could have happened if that train had suddenly lurched while you were under there. You could have been killed. My friends will all know about it. They're going to think your mama's not raising you right."

In my mind, I could just hear one of those phone calls, "Now Vada, you know I try to mind my own business, but I saw Elsie Jane's girl, her name's Carolyn, right? I saw her and the Land girls crawl under the train this afternoon. Yes, crawled right under it to the other side. Ordinarily, I wouldn't tell on kids, but, my goodness, they could have been killed. Well, I just thought you all ought to know." My grandmother, bless her heart, just stood there, looking at me with a sorrowful face, and cried,

"You could have been killed." About this time Uncle Fred showed up from the post office and put his two cents in, "Damn fool thing to have done. You could have been killed." I was beginning to be sorry that I wasn't.

Tears were already flowing when Mama told me to go get the switch. I knew where it was. It was on top of the refrigerator where it stayed my entire childhood. She switched my bare legs. I cried, Grandma cried, and Mama cried as she afterward daubed camphonique on my scratched legs. Aunt Vada busied herself at the stove with her back turned and Uncle Fred retired to the outhouse with the Arkansas Democrat.

They didn't give me bread and water that night, but I was not allowed to eat at the table. Instead, I was banished to the back porch, where I ate by myself on the back step, balancing a plate on my knees, nursing both my scratched legs and a bruised ego. After a spit bath I was sent to bed where I cried myself to sleep.

The next morning Mama hugged me and said, "Carolyn Jane, I may not always love what you do, but I will always love you." She said that to me more than once when I was bad during my growing up years, and I was bad, especially in my young teens. And to her dying day, she loved me so much, and I had the comfort of knowing it. I like to think she loves me still.

P.S. I'll always wonder if Eldon Watson made one of those phone calls.

RED, WHITE AND BARBEQUE

When I was growing up, Portia, Arkansas was the premier place to be in the whole wide world, especially on the Fourth of July. It was time for the Portia Picnic! The whole town was alive with activity and excitement. Why, people all over the state knew about the Portia Picnic. Plans were made to be there. Car after car stirred up the dust on the hot Arkansas roads as they made their way to Portia. Who in their right mind would want to miss the Portia Picnic? Not I.

The picnic took place in the grove adjacent to the elementary school. The Grove was the ideal place for a large gathering. The ancient trees offered shade with ample room underneath the trees to set up all the stands. The nearby school cafeteria was used as a staging area for all the food that was sold in the stands. The school outhouses were convenient and the pump in the schoolyard offered cool water if you had spent all your nickels and needed a drink or needed to wash the sticky off your hands from the cotton candy.

Anchoring one end of the Grove was the speakers' platform. It was bedecked with faded red, white and blue bunting, sported a few straight-backed chairs and a small table with a pitcher of water and a couple of glasses. I don't remember a sound system. Arkansas politicians in those days had to have a strong voice. There were no chairs for an audience to sit on. People just gathered "round. If it was an election year, all the candidates for governor would show up sometime during the picnic and make a stump speech to the eager crowd. The leading candidate was expected to make an appearance at the Portia Picnic on the Fourth of July. Politics in Arkansas was always somewhat of a contact sport so the candidates always drew a crowd. Some came to cheer, and some came to jeer. There was never a Republican candidate, just varieties of Democrat. Heck, most people in Arkansas had never even met a Republican, much less voted for one. They would rather have voted for Hitler. And there were no women candidates, either. Women were thought to have no place in the courthouse or the statehouse, unless they could type.

If it was an off year, the current Governor of the great State of Arkansas always came to the picnic and made a speech. The Governor put on a good show, arriving in a mini convoy of three cars. A State Police car led the way, followed by the Governor's big shiny black sedan with another not-quite-as-grand sedan bringing up the rear. The Governor would burst from his car, glad-handing everybody, kissing babies, greeting people like they were his long- lost brothers/sisters. There was always a big, burly, red-faced State Trooper following on the

Governor's heels. The Governor wore the "uniform" of suit pants, white shirt, and open collar. No suit coat and no tie. It was hot and he was a man of the people who had better sense than to dress up in a suit on the Fourth of July. And he always wiped his brow with a big white handkerchief. I remember one year that the Governor showed up about three sheets in the wind. I suspect that he had already been to umpty-jillion local picnics and had accepted one too many cool libations enhanced with alcohol. He was feeling no pain, gave his rousing speech and sped off to yet another gathering. Some thought it a shame for such a fine man to let himself get in that shape and some thought it just showed, hell, the governor was just like the rest of us.

Politics aside, the real star of the picnic was the barbeque. Whole hogs or at least large chunks of them were lovingly tended in long pits situated between the back of the schoolhouse and the fence that marked the edge of the Grove. The cooks, all men, earnestly worked long hot hours to make the best barbeque, bar none, in the known world.

I don't know how one gained entry into this exclusive fraternity of barbequers. Perhaps it required a legacy, perhaps you just had to know the right people or be in the right place at the right time when a vacancy occurred. At any rate, it was a lifetime commitment and a fierce honor. Only extreme old age or death was an excuse to leave. The merely old brought straight-backed chairs and sat around the pit and offered comments and advice to the active barbequers. Children were not encouraged to venture into this part of the grove. We looked on from afar.

Now, world-class barbeque does not happen in a day, or even two. Great effort was expended far in advance to come up with the perfect pigs. Hickory wood had to be cut and dried, hogs had to be raised and slaughtered. The pit had to be dug out. Since it was in the same spot every year that wasn't hard. Still, it was a big pit. Digging it out was probably a three- beer effort on the part of several young men.

Hickory logs were laid in the pit and the fire started well in advance. The coals had to be deep and hot in the pit, requiring the better part of two days of burning before it was considered ready to receive the pork. The hogs were wrapped in wet burlap, placed on the coals, then more coals were heaped on top and the whole thing covered over with dirt. I don't know how they knew when it was ready, but they did. Part of the charm of the whole thing was the finesse and mystery of the process.

Ah! but when it was deemed cooked to perfection, the hogs were unearthed and prepared. The meat fell off the bone. It was shredded and placed in big pans and set out for sale. Word spread quickly that it was time and a line formed with people carrying containers in which to take it home for supper. Some folks didn't wait, they ate their barbeque right there on the grounds at the picnic tables scattered under the trees. If you were lucky, you got to eat there and at home that night.

Other food items to go with the barbeque were for sale in the various stands throughout the Grove. Additional barbeque sauce, coleslaw, baked beans, potato salad plus desserts of all kinds were all offered. No one had to cook that day.

The stands also offered other things like cotton candy, lemonade, and homemade preserves, jellies, and pickles, sweet and dill. Some ladies sold handmade articles like fancy embroidered pillow cases and tea towels, cute little girl dresses, baby clothes, and knitted sweaters. If somebody made it and was proud of their efforts, they probably sold it at the picnic. Extra money coming in was much appreciated in most Portia households.

There was no fireworks display but we could buy sparklers to light at home after it got dark. Sometimes after supper there was home churned ice cream. If Aunt Vada had time and ice, she'd mix up some ice cream and either my daddy or Uncle Charlie would crank the churn. When it got hard to turn the crank, one of them always said, "Carolyn, come sit on this thing and hold it down for me." Your bottom gets really cold when you're sitting on an ice cream churn, but it was totally worth it.

The Portia Picnic wasn't all about barbeque and politics. It was a time of community. Kids ran all over the place, playing hide and seek or tag or just getting in the way. Old folks who didn't get out as much anymore sat together and caught up on the news, okay, gossip. Young folks flirted with each other, new babies were introduced and people struck up conversations with folks they didn't know as well as they would like, trading observations and maybe making a connection, like, " George Little is my second cousin on my mother's side. Doesn't he live down the road from you?" The farmers always talked about the crops, good and bad. After all, farming was what made the world go around in Northeast Arkansas.

The Picnic was not the fanciest nor the biggest nor the most famous. What it was, was homegrown and genuine. The whole community put aside their differences and came together to honor our country and have a good time. Oh, yes, and to eat the best barbeque in the land.

ON OUR WAY

Our wait was almost over. Mama got travel orders from the Army. It was November. We had been in Portia since May. The deal was, dependents couldn't travel until there were quarters available. Someone was coming home so we could go and take their place. We would soon be on our way.

Part of traveling to Japan was that we had to have shots—lots of them. Not my favorite thing since my reaction to the smallpox vaccine I got while we were still in Brooklyn was a severe, red, swollen, itchy arm. Not something I wanted to repeat. Well, guess what? I did. The shots were spread out over the Fall, administered by Dr. Webb in his office, which was really his converted garage. Everything was OK until it was time for the typhus shot. I don't know how bad actually having typhus is, but the shot to prevent it is a killer. It was a repeat of the smallpox vaccine, only worse. My little skinny arm was swollen and red and oozed pus all the way around—and it hurt! Later I would have booster shots but they didn't behave like the first one. Thank heavens!

We also had to have a passport. Then, as now, you can't get a passport without a birth certificate. I had one, no problem. Mama didn't have one. She was born at home. No doctor attended her birth. I'm guessing that she was delivered by her grandmother, an aunt, or a local midwife or all three. Anyway, no one registered her birth. Well, she had to have some way to prove that she was who she said she was. We went to the courthouse in Walnut Ridge, to the County Clerk's office. They solved the problem easily. They called in Uncle Bill. Bill Archer was married to my grandmother's sister, Aunt Maude. He was the County Judge, a real mover and shaker in Lawrence County.

The clerk asked, "Do you know this woman? Is she Elsie Jane Lane Hornbuckle?"

He laughed, "Hell, yes, that's Elsie Jane."

"How do you know this?" said the clerk.

"Hell, I was in the next room when she was born. I heard her first cry."

"That's good enough. Sign this, please."

"Thank you, Judge."

He gave us both hugs and was gone. The paperwork was done, and that was it, proving the old adage my daddy always quoted,

"It's not what you know, but who you know."

We went down the street to a photographer's studio and had our picture taken. I didn't get my own passport. Instead, I traveled on Mama's so we had our picture taken together. In a couple of weeks, the passport came and we were good to go.

I'm not sure exactly when we left. It had to have been sometime in November, 1949. Maybe the first or second week of the month. We caught the train in Hoxie. Everyone was there to see us off. I often wonder what they thought, the family, since we were going to live in a country that had lately been our enemy. "Where the heathens worship idols." That from my grandmother. Additionally, the Japanese had claimed the life of one of their own, a son of one of the Lane sisters, one of Mama's cousins. He died in a POW camp somewhere around Tokyo. While we were there, Mama and Daddy searched and found the location of the camp. I don't know if he was buried there or if his body was shipped home. Their report of the visit must have offered some closure for the family. Whatever the family thought, whatever lay ahead, we were on our way. Goodbyes were said. There were some tears and forced smiles. The family, Aunt Vada, Uncle Fred, Grandmother Lane, and Tommy all stood on the platform until we were out of sight.

The train stopped briefly in Poplar Bluff, Mo. where we were met by my other set of grandparents, the Hornbuckles, Cora and Lem. Grandmother Hornbuckle had prepared a picnic for us. I remember fried chicken and potato salad in a jar. There were probably pickles and white bread and some of her pound cake. She made delicious pound cake! More goodbyes, more tears. "Give Charlie a big hug from us when you see him." Then we were off again. The train took us to Union Station in St. Louis where we changed trains for one headed west, all the way to Seattle. I can't remember if we spent one or two nights on the train. I think it was two. What I do remember is lying in the bottom berth, looking out the window as we went through small towns, hearing the train whistle blow at the railroad crossings and seeing the lights of the sleeping towns.

When we got to Seattle, we were housed in a barracks with all the other dependents on their way to Japan, too. I guess we were there a few days. Long enough to go to the PX for some last-minute shopping. Mama bought a picture postcard of Mt. Rainer which she later had an unknown Japanese artist copy into a big oil painting which hangs in my house now as it always did in hers. We must have left around the middle of November. I remember how excited we all were as we took the bus to the port to board the ship, the USS E.D. Patrick. There were three ships that carried dependents and soldiers from Seattle to Tokyo. Besides the USS E.D. Patrick there was the USS M. M. Patrick, known as the Mickey Mouse Patrick, and another one whose name was the USS Mann, as in "Man, oh Mann!" The kids always asked the newcomers, "What boat did you come over on?" "Yeah, well, I came on the XYX, that one's better." Whatever. I don't really remember actually getting on the boat, but I do remember being awakened in the early morning by the sound of the anchor being raised and feeling the movement of the ship as it moved out to sea.

Our stateroom was rather militarily plain. There was one small porthole, bunk beds-berths-one straight-backed chair, a small metal chest of drawers and a small bathroom. No tub, just a shower. Our suitcases slid across the floor with the movement of the ship, as did the chair. Everything else was bolted to the floor. Evidently the Navy only buys gray paint because everything was gray--the furniture, the walls, the floors, the ceiling. There was no closet. The door, gray metal, was heavy and watertight. On the very stormy days we could see the waves wash over the port hole and we were really high up in the ship! Scary! Once, on one of the big rolls, the whole ship shuttered. We were told that the propeller came out of the water. Really scary!!

We were at sea thirteen days, many of them stormy. That ship really rocked and rolled! Everyone was initially seasick. Seasick is carsick, only worse. The car can stop so you can throw up on the side of the road. The ship doesn't stop, it just keeps rolling along. Not everyone made it to the bathroom in time. That made the companionways disgusting and dangerous until one of the old salts on the crew, who also found themselves unexpectedly seasick, could bring themselves to clean it up. Ugh! A story went around that one of the daddies got his hand caught in the door and it cut off his little finger which lay in the companionway for three days before anyone had the stomach to pick it up. I believed it at the time.

The kids recovered first. Because the adults were still in their bunks, the kids pretty much were on their own. We roamed the ship, making friends and having adventures. There were movies in the theater but because it was so rough, the chairs were taken out and we sat on the floor, sliding back and forth across the floor with the rolling of the ship. That was fun! After the sea calmed down a little, we were allowed on deck to watch the ocean roll. Once we saw whales swimming by. We were forbidden to attend the ceremony/party when we crossed the International Date Line. It was adults only. Judging from the look on Mama's face when she got back, she was not much impressed with King Neptune and his antics. She would much rather have been in the lounge where there were comfortable chairs and bridge tables. Didn't matter. I was probably playing with my new friends, the Williams sisters.

When people got so they could eat and keep it down, we ate in the mess hall or whatever they call a dining room on a ship. We had assigned tables. The tables all had an edge on them. Took me a while to figure out why that edge was there. A few rolls of the ship and I knew that it was there to keep the plates from sliding off the table. By the way, the table was bolted to the floor, too. Mama and I shared a table with the Williams family — Mrs. Williams (can't remember her first name), Marjorie, one year older, Carolyn Sue, one year younger, and little brother Tommy. They were from West Tennessee. I think Mama thought they were hicks from the sticks. Takes one to know one, but this Arkansas girl had lived in New Your City and I guess she thought that gave her a leg up. Anyway, we girls all became fast friends, exploring the ship and trying to avoid having Tommy tag along.

We must have celebrated Thanksgiving on that passage over the Pacific, but I don't remember it. Everyone was probably still seasick so it most likely was a non-event. Turkey, dressing, and cranberry sauce don't go well with being seasick. But time passed and so did the seasickness. We ended up enjoying the last few days of the voyage. Finally, we arrived in the port of Tokyo. It was December 3rd, 1949. I remember seeing my daddy on the pier looking eagerly for us as we docked. Living in Portia, Arkansas had been wonderful.

Only later would I realize the magic of those days. Now it was time for new adventures in the Land of the Rising Sun.

FUJI VIEW

We had arrived, and survived, our thirteen-day voyage across the stormy Pacific. My father, and all the fathers, were there, as the ship docked, waving, and shouting a greeting. I remember searching the crowd for him as he was searching the passengers crowded on the rail of the ship for us. We waved when we finally saw him. I was so happy to see my daddy! He left Arkansas in June and it was now December 3rd, 1949. That was a long time. Daddy came aboard and there were big old hugs and kisses all around. The ship was fairly radiating joy. Everyone was happy to be reunited. Hugs, kisses, handshakes, back slaps, and even a few tears were all around us. We met Mr. Williams briefly, and said a temporary good-by to the Williams family. They were going to the same place we were, so we would catch up with them later.

But we had just arrived. There were things to do to get settled. We were not going to permanent quarters right away. We were to stay up in the mountains above Tokyo at the Fuji View Hotel. This was a Japanese resort that the Occupation Forces had taken over. It would be the first way station in our journey to permanent quarters.

The first order of business was to get my schoolbooks so our first stop was the School Board Office. There was no school at the Fuji View. The mothers were expected to teach their children. Home schooling was not a current term yet but that was what it was. We picked up the proper books and headed up the mountain to the Fuji View Hotel.

On the way out of Yokohama, we drove through what must have been acres of bombed-out buildings. The streets had been cleared so traffic could move, but everything else was just bits and pieces of buildings—homes, stores, offices, all burned and in ashes. There were a few intact buildings, but not many. There was life in the ruins, though. People had built shanties in the midst of the destruction. They had taken what remained of those buildings and constructed a place for them to live. I had never seen anything like it. People had to live that way?

"What happened here ?," I asked. "Why are all the houses broken?"

"They were bombed," my daddy said.

"Why? Why would you do that to people's houses?"

"Because we were at war with the Japanese." "But that's not nice. They didn't bomb our house." "It was war, Carolyn. That's the way wars are fought." My   eight-year-old self was getting an education in what war looks like from the ground up. I will never forget those sights.

All the way out of Yokohama and into the countryside, it was the same. Bombed out buildings everywhere. There were a few structures still standing but nothing was in good shape. As the country got more rural, things began to change. There was still damage, but not as much. We passed thatched-roofed farmhouses that seemed not to have doors but walls that slid open so you could come in. There were kitchen gardens out back, farm animals in pens, the usual farm stuff, only different. Oh, but there were chickens in the yards. That was the only thing like Arkansas. No tractors, nothing mechanized. As we climbed into the hills, the rice patties started to climb the hills, too. They were terraced up the side of the hills in little bitty increments, thin fields following the contour of the hills with low walls of dirt to hold the water needed for the rice. There were rice patties on the flat areas, too, but evidently there was not enough flat land to grow enough to meet the needs of the people so the fields climbed the hills.

As the road got steeper, it also narrowed until we were climbing the side of the mountain on a one-lane road clinging to its side. Every once in a while, there was a wide place in the road. Daddy said that if you met a car coming down, one of the cars had to back up to the nearest wide place so the cars could pass. I was more than a little worried, but we made it all the way to the top.

The Fuji View Hotel was a grand hotel. There was a circular drive to the impressive double front doors complete with a covered portico. In the curve of the drive was a large tall fountain. The hotel was three stories high with a large lobby and not one, but two, dining rooms, plus a bar and, I think, multiple card rooms. Very grand.

We checked in and took the elevator to our rooms. We had two adjoining rooms, plus a private bathroom. Mama didn't like the arrangements much because I was not sleeping in the same room, but she tolerated it for it gave she and Daddy privacy on the weekends. They were typical hotel rooms, just like in the States, with one big difference—the view. Our windows looked out across a large lake and up to Mt. Fuji which was nothing if not magnificent. It loomed over the hotel like the big, beautiful presence that it was. The flat top was covered with snow. It is supposed to be an inactive volcano but it sometimes looked as if smoke was coming out of the top. It was really just blowing snow.

We settled in and went downstairs to the dining room. The Williams family was there, too. I was glad to see my friends. Turned out their rooms were just down the hall from ours. This was going to be great! Our meal was nice. It was American food. All the staff in the hotel were Japanese. They looked a little different, but they were nice and polite. Their English was funny. The only other people I had ever heard speak funny English with an accent were the Brooklynites back in the States. We sat in the lobby and talked a while, then went upstairs to bed. All the residents of the hotel were newly arrived dependents waiting for quarters to become available in Tokyo or Yokohama, so we knew people from our boat. On weekends, the husbands/fathers came up but during the week it was just the wives and kids.

Now, what did we do? No one had to cook or clean. We ate in the dining room and our beds were made when we got back to the room. Our dirty clothes disappeared and came back clean and ironed. Oh, yes. School. Mama was supposed to teach me but her heart just wasn't in it. She had not graduated from high school but she was smart. Certainly, smart enough to teach me. We started where we had left off. She was teaching me to write cursive, something I had missed as I bounced around from school to school, even though I did get a few lessons in Portia.

Mama wrote a good hand. The problem was translating writing from her right hand to my left hand. With practice, I did learn to write, but I think it looks funny. I was given spelling words to learn. And I read to Mama from my English book. She told me the words I didn't know. We kind of skipped over arithmetic and grammar, though I was still working on learning the multiplication tables. They were not fun. Arithmetic was left to Daddy on the weekends. I did learn to count on my fingers. Still do.

Afternoons were recess. We were free to do whatever we wanted as long as we didn't get into too much trouble. Our moms took naps, read books, and played bridge. The kids, and there were a lot of us, explored the hotel and its grounds. We made friends with the staff. The Japanese are very forgiving of their children up to a certain age. Since we weren't that age yet, we pretty much did all sorts of things we would not have been able to get away with in the States. Like push the big laundry carts in a race up and down the halls and play race with the elevators. We would push the button on the elevator and then run up, or down, the stairs to see if we could beat it to the next floor. We were, after all, Army Brats.

Then it snowed. Oh, my goodness! It really snowed serious snow, feet, not inches. We couldn't wait to bundle up and get out and play in the snow. It was so deep! It had snowed in Brooklyn, but not like this. It was taller than me in some places. We had snowball fights, made snowmen by the dozen, and even built a few snow forts. There was a recreation office where we could get skies and sleds. I had never seen skies. Fortunately, there weren't any steep hills, just gentle slopes. We skied and sledded down the slopes, then made snow angels followed by hot chocolate at the hotel bar.

Christmas was coming. The lobby was graced with a tall, beautifully decorated Christmas tree. We even had a small tabletop tree in Mama's room. There were a few handmade ornaments, but no lights. The best thing about Christmas at the Fuji View Hotel was the fountain in the circular drive out front. A tall pine tree was positioned on top of the fountain and the water turned on. The water shot up the tree and froze into jillions of sparkly icicles all over it. It was beautiful!

Daddy gave me some money to buy Mama a Christmas present. The only place to shop was the gift shop in the basement of the hotel. It was stocked with Japanese dishes and do-dads, most of which were a mystery to me. I shopped and shopped. I finally decided on a set of three cloisonné salt cellars complete with tiny silver spoons. Mama maybe used them once, but they were always in the China cabinet. That Christmas was not big on presents. Santa Claus did come. He brought me some new slippers and a horse racing board game. Mama and Daddy exchanged presents. I surely got Daddy something but I don't remember what it was. This Christmas was more about family and being together. That was the best gift of all.

We did get a little extra gift that Christmas, if you want to call it a gift. It was the weekend. Daddy was there.

Mama was still in bed and Daddy was lounging in his pj's in a chair by the window. I was playing on the floor and just listening to them talk. Then there was a loud thump, and everything started shaking. Our little Christmas tree almost fell off the table.

Mama yelled, "Charles, what was that?"

"It's just a little earthquake, don't worry."

Then there was an aftershock. Mama jumped out of bed. "What should we do? I'm not dressed."

"Nothing, it's over. There's nothing to worry about."

Then there was yet another, smaller aftershock.

"Oh, Lord! We should get out of here. Carolyn, get my purse. Where are your shoes? Charles, do something"

He did something. He laughed. "Elsie Jane, it's over. We're fine."

She didn't believe him. How could everything be fine when the whole building, the whole earth, was shaking? She made us all get dressed and at least leave the third floor and go down to the dining room for breakfast. And she made sure to take her purse. This was by no means the last earthquake we would experience, but it was the most fun, at least, I thought so.

For Christmas dinner, the hotel went all out. There was a huge buffet laid out in the dining room, candles on the tables. Additionally, there was candy in fancy bowls, little trees, ornaments, greenery, the whole nine yards. The Japanese were doing their best to make us feel at home. I don't know if the Japanese management read up on Western customs or if they were guided, or misguided, by Occupation personnel, but their efforts lost a little in translation. In the center of the buffet table were a roast turkey and a roast duck. Both the birds, and they were BIG, were presented on large silver platters decorated with appropriate greenery around their bodies. The only thing was, they both still had their heads! And the heads were erect, like they were looking around, scanning the crowd, asking, "What happened?" The sight of them was shocking, then funny, then just weird. How do you react when the intention is certainly good, but the results certainly are not? Families retired to their tables and tried not to look at the main course staring at them. Eventually, the fowls were carved and served, much to everyone's relief. Everything else was good, though.

One day after Christmas Mama and I went exploring in a little village that was close to the hotel. There was a house under construction so we decided to go in and poke around. There was a kitchen, not like ours, but you could tell it was a place meant for cooking. The house was pretty open, but it was obvious that there would be sliding walls to make different rooms. No closets. Where was the bathroom? We found it. Down a small hall there was a room with a hole in the floor. That was it. Well, OK. It was basically an outhouse built in the house. What did they do with the poop? There was no deep hole like in the outhouses in Portia.

The mystery was solved later when Daddy told us about honey buckets. Honey buckets were large wooden buckets held together with two strands of thick rope around them. They had a wooden lid and a big scoop. The honey bucket went under the hole in the floor to catch the poop. Then where did the poop go? Ahh, that's when it got interesting. The poop went on the fields as fertilizer. Really? Mama was horrified. We certainly were never going to eat anything that came out of a Japanese field if that was the best they could do for fertilizer. And we never did. Not knowingly, anyway. Except when I cheated and bought stuff from the food carts on Avenue D.

I really don't remember just when we left Fuji View. It was probably sometime in late January, 1950. Our next stop was in Yokohama, but not in permanent quarters yet. We were assigned to half a Quonset hut in a temporary quarters compound of maybe twenty other Quonset huts. Later, in the Spring, we would move to permanent quarters.

In the meantime, we were learning about Japanese culture. Mama had a phrase book. We learned to say Please—Dozo, and Thank You—Arigato gozimas. And to expect a bow instead of a handshake. I learned to eat with chopsticks. We learned all sorts of things that made us not of the culture but at least in it a little bit.

QUONSET HUT LIVING

Our time at the Fuji View Hotel was over. We moved down to Yokohama. This was yet another transition, this time from a luxury hotel to half a Quonset hut. We were on our way to permanent quarters, but not quite yet.

The living accommodations were a step down, to say the least. Our temporary quarters in that half of a Quonset hut were tight. Each half had a furnished living room with a small kerosene stove, one bedroom, one bathroom, and a "hall." There was a window in the living room and a small one in the bathroom. The master bed was made from packing crates. I think Mama and Daddy had a small chest of drawers. No closet. My bed was a standard issue Army cot in the hall under a set of shelves, meant, I guess, to take the place of a closet. There was no kitchen. We ate in the Mess Hall down the street.

If the living arrangements were a step down, daily living was a step up. First and foremost, Daddy was living with us full time. That was the best thing. I got to see him every day. I also started back to real school. The kids were bussed to Nasugbu Beach Elementary School. It was early

February, so I did the last part of the third grade again, which I had already done in Portia. Oh, well.

Nasugbu Beach School was a far cry from P.S. 102 in Brooklyn and an even farther cry from Portia Elementary School. Before the war, it had been a Japanese Girls' School. Now it housed grades one through eight of Occupation Army brats who were taught by American teachers imported from the States. Sometimes Japanese teachers would come to observe how Americans educated their young. Since I am left-handed, it was not unusual for a visiting teacher to gently take the pencil from my left hand and put it in my right. Evidently you are not allowed to be left-handed in Japan.

The school was a large three story, rectangular stucco building surrounded by playing fields. There was a playground at one end. Kids from Area 1 and Area 2 attended the school. Most of the Area 2 kids rode the bus to school while all the Area 1 kids walked. The school was just inside the Area 2 gate off Avenue D. Little did I know when I first started there that I would end up living up the hill from the school and would have to be among the very few Area 2 kids who had to walk to school.

Also, I celebrated my ninth birthday while we lived in the Quonset hut. After school, there was a party in the Mess Hall. All my friends came and the cook even baked me a birthday cake with "Happy Birthday, Carolyn!" on it. I got presents. We played games. I thought it was pretty special. How many kids do you know who had a birthday party in a mess hall?

We were also assigned a Japanese maid. This was part of the Occupation's effort to employ the Japanese and get the economy up and running again. When we were finally assigned permanent quarters, the maid made the move with us. Yokusa-san was a nice young girl who spoke passing English. What I remember most about her was her act of kindness. We were still in the Quonset hut. One morning she came in with a small, rectangular container much like a sardine tin. She opened it up and proudly showed it to my mama. Inside were five sushi rolls that her mother had made for us. Typical sushi rolls, they were filled with rice and raw fish and wrapped in seaweed. Mama probably had never heard of, much less seen, sushi rolls. And she was still reeling from the discovery of honey buckets and how their contents were used.

It was a beautiful presentation that probably took some time and effort. Mama thanked her and said that she would wait until Papa-san got home to try them. The girl was gone when Daddy got home. They opened the tin and carefully examined the contents, Mama gingerly poking the rolls with her finger. "I don't know, Charles. Is the fish raw? Have you ever seen seaweed? Do we dare eat it? The final answer was a resounding "No." It was a hard decision to make since the offering was well-intentioned.

They sent me to the Mess Hall to throw it away there so Yokusa-san wouldn't know it wasn't eaten. The next day Mama sent a written thank-you note with the admonition to please don't go to all that trouble again.

Our time living in the hut was short, probably just six or so weeks. I was ready to go to a real house with a real bed, not the cot I had been sleeping on. I'm sure Mama was ready for a real house to call her own. We had arrived in early December and it was now coming on Spring. Our ultimate destination was to be #331 Area 2. Couldn't wait to get there!

331# AREA 2

Finally! We were to move to permanent quarters. The one-half Quonset hut with no kitchen was to be a thing of the past. We were to live in Area 2. In a real, American-style house. Area 1, another housing area, was across Avenue D, the Yokohama main drag, on the flat land that was closer to Tokyo Bay. It housed about 125 families. Area 2 had a little over 400 houses. It was in the hills, mostly. Entrance to both areas was through a gate which had a guard house manned by MPs day and night. Nasugbu Beach School was on the right as you entered the Area 2 gate. Areas 1 and 2 shared the school, also Nasugbu Beach Chapel, half way up the hill, and the Nasugbu Beach shopping center.

The shopping center fronted Ave. D and had a small PX with a covered outdoor café, a movie theater, a library, a fire station, a bowling alley, offices for something which I do not remember, and a cop house for the MPs. There was a gas station (13 cents a gallon!) complete with a full-service garage. In Area 1 there was a community center that had a ball room, a kitchen, and a playing field. This was where, among other things, the Girl Scouts and Boy

Scouts met, lots of bridge was played, ballet lessons held, and softball played.

The road went up a steep hill just past the school. About a third of the way up was a small outcrop on the side of the hill where our houses were. A sharp left turn took you into our little area. There were about a dozen houses built around a street in the shape of a question mark. All the houses looked alike except they were different colors—either light green, light blue, or light beige. Mostly, the back doors faced the street. Our house, like all the others, had a small kitchen, an L-shaped living room and dining room, three bedrooms, and one bathroom. There was a small covered front porch and a concrete back stoop, with, for some reason, an ice box next to it. We had a refrigerator in the kitchen so I do not know why it was there, but it was and we regularly got a delivery of blocks of ice. No garage, all cars parked on the street.

There were sidewalks, streetlights, and grass in the yards. I don't remember any landscaping, no shrubbery, no flower beds. Maybe someone would put a small pot of flowers on the front porch. That was it. The grass was tended by a crew of squatting Japanese men who cut the grass with hand clippers. Later I remember a push mower being used. But the grass crew did not change. One guy pushed the mower and the rest of the crew trimmed a little around the houses and them sat and watched the guy push the mower. I guess they switched at some point. There were no trees anywhere. There was some bamboo growing on the side of the hill. The best feature of the house was the view. Out our living room windows we could see Mt. Fuji. It loomed on the horizon every day that it was not cloudy. We could see the snow on the summit wax and wane with the seasons. We could see the wind blow the snow into white, fluffy clouds. Not everyone gets to grow up with a Mt. Fuji view.

Now, we came to Japan with just our clothes. We were not allowed to bring anything else. The Army was to provide everything we would need. When it was time to move to Area 2, Mama and Daddy went to a big Government Housing warehouse and picked out everything, from a very limited choice, furniture, rugs, kitchen essentials, linens, and dishes and a washing machine. No dryer, there was a clothesline in the yard. No pictures, no do-dads. If we wanted those, we would have to provide them.

The furniture was a little "beachy", rattan with colorful tropical print cushions. Certainly not what we were used to and certainly not anything my parents would have chosen if they had had a choice. We had two side chairs, a couch, side tables, a coffee table, and a dining room table with six chairs and a China cabinet. I think there was a floor lamp and maybe table lamps, which were soon replaced with much prettier Japanese lamps. There were two unmatched rugs in the living room and dining room but nowhere else. There were hardwood floors. I was wrong about thinking I would have a real bed. Sure 'nuf, my bed was made from packing crates. I think Mama and Daddy's was, too. We could not put anything under the beds, and I could not hide under the bed if I did anything wrong and wanted to disappear. I do seem to remember that the bed in the master bedroom had a drawer. Of course, each bedroom had a closet, but the doors were different. They were sliding doors. We had never seen anything like that. They are common now, but not then. I guess we stole the idea from the Japanese.

Later we acquired a bar/liquor cabinet, a gift from the Japanese men who worked for Daddy. It was made of Philippine mahogany, rectangular, taller than a table, with double doors on the front of the cabinet. The sides were angled, making shelves to hold glasses. The top lifted to disclose a mirror. It was pretty, but not something we used much. I remember reading my mother's expression when the men carried it through the door. "What on earth are we going to do with this thing?" Contrary to what most Japanese seemed to think, not all Americans are drinkers and therefore do not need a bar. Most of the time, all I remember was a bottle of bourbon kept, not in the bar, but way under the sink. We were mostly Coca-Cola people.

The other item of furniture we got was a display case for my collection of dolls. Daddy designed it. It, too, was made of Philippine mahogany with a special shelf for my tall geisha doll and other shelves for the rest of the collection. The glass door was so heavy that it had to be propped up when the case was open or the whole thing would tip over. It was put together with pretty brass fittings. I already had some dolls, the story-book kind. But Mama bought me Japanese dolls. I had the tall, elegant geisha, the Emperor and Empress, a Samurai warrior, a dancer with a drum, a housewife and her farmer husband. Later, Daddy would bring me dolls from his trips to Korea. And later still, dolls from Greenland. Much later still, the dolls were put away and I used it as a bookcase.

Like all kids, school was the most important thing in my life. Because we lived close to school, and because a school bus could never have made that sharp left turn, we walked, or rather descended and ascended, to school. There were six or seven of us who trekked up and down the what seemed like a million concrete steps interspersed with small landings, to the foot of the hill and across the road to school. We went down in the morning, up and back down at noon, and up again after school. There was usually a kind MP who made sure we crossed the busy road safely.

I liked school. I liked my teachers. I had a bunch of friends. School was fun. The playground could be a lot of fun, too. It had the usual swings, a slide, a couple of see-saws and, for want of a better term, a maypole. Something no school principal currently would ever allow because there was potential for disaster. The maypole had hand grips attached on the ends of eight long chains which were attached to a rotating gear at the top of a tall pole. Like all maypoles, you ran in a circle around it. The difference was that instead of wrapping pretty ribbons around the pole, if you got going fast enough, you could leave the ground and swing high in the air. Just be sure to hold on tight. It was so much fun! We played dodge ball, Red Rover, hopscotch and chase the boys/girls. That's how I broke my arm. The boy I was about to catch stopped and squatted down and I sailed right over him, landing on my right arm. At the hospital, the doctor put a cast on it which everyone signed, including the offending boy. When it was taken off, I wanted to keep it, but Mama said no.

Once, the three stories of the school building were used to an interesting advantage. There had been a small earthquake, centered in Tokyo Bay. This caused a small tsunami to develop. Since the school building was so tall, it would be possible to see the tsunami from the roof. The whole school was ushered to the roof to see the tsunami roll in. It was just this big, white wave that rocked a lot of boats as it came ashore, but did no real damage. Not all tsunamis are that benign. It was neat!

Like all schools, we had safety drills, not just fire drills, but earthquake drills, and, after the Korean War got started and was going badly, air raid drills. The air raid drills were, "Get under your desk, cover your head with your arms, and face away from the windows." The earthquake and fire drills were designed to get us out of the building as fast as possible. "Form a line, don't run, don't push, walk through the hall as far away from the windows as possible, and when you get outside, move away from the building."

As the Korean War progressed, the Army required all children to memorize our father's serial number. I still remember Daddy's—O348067. In case of an emergency, we needed some way to identify our fathers. They wore dog tags, we did not. This was when it was not unimaginable that the Chinese would take the war to Japan and conduct air raids on Tokyo and Yokohama. After all, at some point, they were almost pushing the Marines off the Korean peninsula at Pusan. At home, Mama had to have a 5-gallon jerry can of fresh water, changed monthly, a first-aid kit, a stash of C-rations, and something else I cannot remember, maybe extra shoes and clothes.

At school, usually during afternoon recess, a small plane would fly over the school. Someone got the idea that it was probably a North Korean or Chinese reconnaissance plane spying on us. Well, we would have none of that. As it flew over, we would all shake our fists at it and yell insults. Since Haneda Airport was just down the road, it was probably just a plane on some harmless mission.

We all knew that there was a war going on in our backyard and we understood what war could do because we saw destruction all around us. Even though several years had passed since World War II ended, there were still plenty of devastated areas left to remind us of what bombs can do. Additionally, we were aware of the wounded soldiers from Korea in the hospitals and hobbling around on their crutches in the PX and Commissary. Mama volunteered as a Gray Lady in the mental ward of the hospital. She had one patient, a young soldier, who was so traumatized by what he had experienced in Korea, that he spent his days hiding under the bed. Mama said that she would get down on the floor, crawl under the bed, and talk to him for hours. Eventually, he was transferred to the States. She always wondered how he fared.

There was a little bonus to having the Korean War nearby. Bob Hope came to call! He was on his way to do USO shows in Korea and stopped off in Tokyo to do a show. It was in a large outdoor arena somewhere between Yokohama and Tokyo, and it was packed. Everyone wanted to see Bob Hope. I do not remember who the other performers were, but it was a good show. What I remember most, though, were the GIs in wheelchairs down front. We watched them being wheeled in. Some were missing limbs, some had bandages on their heads or over their eyes. Others were on crutches. Just another reminder of where we were and the times in which we lived.

Some of our fathers were involved in the conduct of the Korean War. The mission of the Army of Occupation changed when the Korean War came along. Now they were supporting an actively engaged army just across the Sea of Japan. Just about everything that was destined for Korea went through Japan, specifically, the Port of Yokohama. Men and material all stopped first in Japan, got sorted out, then shipped over to Korea. My father was in the Transportation Corps. His job was to move things where they needed to be. He made many trips to Korea, to check if things got where they were supposed to go. As a bonus, I got to accompany Daddy to the Port, mostly after hours, when he went to check on things. I got to ride on a PT boat out to a big troop ship, wave at a train full of GIs on their way to Korea, visit Haneda Airport and watch the planes get loaded and take off. Daddy always wanted me to know what he did for a living. Other fathers were likewise engaged in supporting the war. We heard their stories and understood that we lived adjacent to a war zone.

But back to Area 2. One day we were playing our way up the hill, (We did not always stay on the steps). I spotted a pile of broken dishes. There was one unbroken plate. It was blue and white, decorated with birds, some scrolling, and some flowers. It was small, maybe four or five inches across. I thought it was pretty. I took it home and proudly showed it to Mama and our maid. Tsudasa-san took one look at it and we knew by the look on her face that something was wrong. She told us that it was the kind of offering plate that is left on Japanese headstones to hold gifts for the dead. Mama put it away. We never used it. We always called it the Dead Plate. I have it still and still do not use it. The speculation was that when our houses were built, what was left of a Japanese cemetery was bulldozed off the top of our little outcropping of the hill, the graves desecrated and lost forever. How sad.

Farther up the hill was Nasugbu Beach Chapel. It was a standard- issue Army Chapel. If you have seen one, you have seen them all. It served both Protestant and Catholic congregations and was overseen by chaplains of both faiths. On Sunday mornings, the Catholics worshipped first, then the Protestants. The congregants greeted one another as they made the transition. There was a Sunday School building, with classrooms and a social hall and offices for the chaplains and their assistants. Protestants had Sunday School while the Catholics celebrated Mass, then we switched, and the Catholics had their Sunday School. The chapel itself had a center aisle, with organ pipes on the front wall. The center aisle led to the high alter with either a Catholic or Protestant cross in the center. After Mass, the Catholics were supposed to exchange their cross with Jesus on it for the Protestant cross without Jesus. Sometimes they forgot and we Protestants worshipped with the Catholic cross still on the alter. Did not seen to make a whole lot of difference.

In the summer, we had Vacation Bible School. At the end of the week, as part of the closing ceremony, the kids would have a Bible drill for the benefit of our parents. The object was to show off how familiar you were with the books of the Bible and how fast you could look up a Bible verse. By the way, the New Testament is easier than the Old. Additionally, we learned the Bible stories and songs. It was fun.

My favorite thing at church was the children's choir. The choir director was a volunteer. She did it because she enjoyed choir. Because she liked it, we liked it, too. She taught us "Be kind to your fine feathered friends, etc., etc. It ends with "You may think that is the end, well, it is." We would hold the issss, and then sing "isn't 'cause there is another chorus." Then we would continue and go another round-or-two-or-three before finally ending it. What fun!

Once a month we sang with the adult choir. We progressed down the center aisle in our fancy collars, usually singing "Savior, Like a Shepherd Lead Us." Once, I asked my friend Linda to join the choir and she came with me to practice. After she had been coming a few weeks, the choir director pulled me aside and told me that Linda did not have what it takes to sing in the choir and she was going to ask her to not come anymore. She hoped that I understood. Well, I did not. I thought we were both being booted out of the choir. I was devastated and burst into tears the minute I walked into the house. Mama knew something was not right about my story so she called the choir director and got the real story. I was still in the choir! Linda was the one who was not. What a relief! Things were a little awkward with Linda at first, but we worked it out, as friends do.

One of the items I left behind in Portia was my bicycle. But soon after arriving in Area 2, I got a new bike. This one was a Japanese bike. The difference between a Japanese bike and an American bike are the tires. Japanese tires are smaller than American tires. This would prove to be a problem when it was time to go back to the States. Daddy said we would never be able to buy new tires in America, so I had to leave it behind. I guess we just left it by the back door for the next kid to ride.

Meanwhile, I could ride my bike. My friend next door, Karen Ikuno, also had a bike, so we often rode together. Karen was a Nisei, a Japanese American. Her parents were both Japanese who grew up in California. I think some of the family may have spent some time in one of the detention camps. But they were out now, and her father was an American Army officer. The problem with Karen and I riding our bikes was that there really was no place to ride. You can only ride around a semi-circle so many times before it gets boring. One day we decided that we would venture out of our neighborhood and ride to the top of the hill. There was a huge water tank at the top that we wanted to see up close. That hill was very steep but we felt sure we could do it. Well, no. We got less than a third of the way to the top and totally gave up. Our little legs just gave out. So, we turned around and decided to coast down the hill, not the best idea, but we did it anyway. So off we went, feet off the pedals, going too fast, barreling into our neighborhood, being careful to veer to the right as we approached our street. That we did not crash is a miracle. Thereafter, we contented ourselves with just cruising our little street.

The Williams sisters, Margie, and Carolyn Sue, whom I met on the ship coming over, were my fast friends. I saw them at school every day. Sometimes I rode the bus home with them after school and sometimes they walked up the steps to my house after school. Additionally, our parents played bridge together often so we were together a lot. We often had to watch Tommy, their little brother, while our parents played cards or our mothers shopped.

One day I was at their house and they showed me into their parents' bedroom, specifically, to their father's bedside table. It is important to note that their mother was not at home. They had found something mysterious, a box of little square plastic packages. Inside each package was a rubber tube. What was it? Did I know? No. Now, they had seen baby Tommy's diaper changed, so they knew what males looked like "down there." I did not. They clued me in. Oh! But after speculation, we decided that it had something to do with their daddy's "thing" and he put the tube on his "thing" when they went to church so if he had to go to the bathroom, he just peed in that thing and emptied it after church. Problem solved. Ah, innocence! But we did flush the one we looked at down the toilet so Mr. Williams would not know we had been snooping.

Another time we walked into their house, took one look at their mother, and knew something was wrong. That, and the maid was not there as she usually was. What had happened was a colossal misunderstanding involving colloquial English. Mrs. Williams had asked the maid to throw out the waste baskets, so she did what Mrs. Williams asked her to do, which was not at all what Mrs. Williams meant. Evidently, when the mistake was discovered, it was too late to rescue the waste baskets which meant all new ones had to be purchased. A prime example of why English is said to be hard to learn.

Everyone had a maid. They were young Japanese women employed by the Army of Occupation to serve the dependent families and to give them income to bolster the Japanese economy. When we first arrived, they were paid by the Army. Later, each family was expected to pay their salary. We had three different maids. The first one came with us from our stay in the Quonset hut village. Then there was an older one, Tusuda-san, who, I think, was considered an "old maid." Her fiancé' had been killed in the war and she had not found anyone else. She was a seamstress, too, and made some of my and my mama's clothes.

The last maid was a teenager, young and pretty. She took me to visit her parents in Tokyo. We took the RTO train from Yokohama. They lived in a typical Japanese house with sliding doors and walls, tatami mats on the floor, low tables, no chairs, and a small alcove with a pretty kakemono hanging on the wall above a small alter with offering plates and candles. Her parents spoke no English but smiled and patted me on the back. About all I could say was arigato, thank you, and dozo, please. But the cultures intersected a little bit and that was a good thing.

Mostly the maid and Mama shared cooking duties. I am not sure the two young ones were cooks, but Tusuda-san was a good cook. She taught Mama how to make fried rice and tempura. The secret to good fried rice is to wash the starch out of the rice before you cook it. That simply involves putting the rice in a bowl of water and swishing it around, changing the water a couple of times until the water is clear. That way, the rice does not stick together when it's cooked. Tempura 's secret is to have the oil very, very hot and the batter very cold. Tusuda-san put ice cubes in the batter so when the vegetables were put in the hot oil, they steamed inside while the outside was nice and crisp.

I do not know why the maids were moved around from family to family. If Mama was ever displeased with one of our maids, I never knew it. The Army just likes to move people, I guess. The maids either stayed at their American families' house or at a maids' barracks up the hill from where we lived. They only got to go home on their day off. I remember one of our maids asked Mama if she could go home to see her father. Mama said, "But you told me your father's dead." "He is, but he will be there. He will come tomorrow night." "But he can't, if he's dead." "Yes, but his spirit will visit us. We will see him. He comes with all the others every year." Mama would not let her go. I thought then and I think now that it was not the right thing to do. Mama really hurt her feelings. I wonder if Mama thought it was the Christian thing to do.

There was no TV. I don't remember a radio, but here must have been one. Probably didn't play anything kids were interested in, so we played outside or played games in each other's rooms. In the winter, when it snowed, and it snowed a lot, we built snowmen and snow forts and had a lot of snowball fights. There was a manhole cover in one of the sidewalks. We found that if we piled snow on the manhole, the heat coming up from it would form a snow cave. How neat was that? We played in the cave until we were frozen, then retreated to someone's house for hot chocolate.

Every kid likes to go barefoot in the summer. All my young life I had ditched my shoes in the summertime. Not so in Japan. The Army had decreed that shoes were to be always worn outdoors, no exceptions. The reason: hookworms. Seems they were in the soil just waiting to hook on to our little feet and cause us harm. The MPs were known to roll slowly by, checking to see if we had on shoes, and yelling at us to put our shoes on if we did not. In the Army, if a kid got in trouble, his daddy also got in trouble, so we were pretty good about wearing shoes.

Well, there are shoes, and then there are geta. Geta are a kind of cross between flipflops and clogs. The straps that hold them on your foot are like flipflops, but the bottoms are flat, made of wood with two clogs about two or three inches high, one toward the front and one toward the back so they held your feet off the ground. We wore them until the clogs were almost worn down to nothing. Then we would go down to the shoe shop on Ave. D and buy another pair.

Besides the Army, my family also had rules, as does every family. One rule I had to follow on pain of death if I did not, was that I was not to refer to the Japanese as "Japs" or "Nips." That rule was right up there with not saying "nigger." Respect was to be given to any and all. That was the Army way and it was our way.

As I had been promised, we had a cat. I do not remember her name, but she was a Manx, stubby tail, funny ears. I loved my kitty. When it was time to go back Stateside, of course, we could not take her with us. Daddy gave her to a Japanese family he knew, probably one of the guys who worked for him. We trusted that they would take care of my cat. There was a delay in leaving and I wanted to visit my cat. Daddy checked to see if we could stop by and see the cat and was told that they no longer had the cat, but they did not say why. Mama always swore they ate her. I certainly hope not, but it was not out of the question.

Avenue D was a commercial street lined with small Japanese shops, one of which was a shoe store. They sold geta and zori. Zori are the flat, fancy-dress shoes covered with fabric meant to be worn for walking around, not playing tag or softball. Next door was the toy store. We called it "Best Toys Easter" because that was the name on the sign when we moved to Area 2. But the name changed with the holidays. It could be "Best Toys Christmas" or "Best Toys Halloween" or "Best Toys 4th", whatever the owners thought would attract the Americans with money to their store. Mama would give me a hundred yen to spend, always saying, "Now, Carolyn, do not pay full price. Jew them down. They expect you to bargain with them." Sometimes I did, sometimes I didn't.

Another thing Mama always said was, "Carolyn, don't buy food down there." This was because she was still horrified about the honey buckets and how the Japanese used the contents of said buckets to fertilize their fields. That made all Japanese food suspect and off limits. Of course, that command did not stop me from buying sesame sticks and candy from the Japanese food carts that were parked along Avenue D. I never got sick, nothing seemed to hurt me. But you can bet that those purchases were a deep, dark secret.

One of the things that went on at school that nobody liked was shots. We all had to have a bunch of shots to get to Japan and now we had to have more. Oh, no! We had to have boosters of Jap B and tetanus and typhoid and typhus and cholera, and, I think, diphtheria and whooping cough. We knew we were in for it when the word got out that we had to bring our shot record to school. The shot record was a long, rectangular document with all the possible shots listed on it. Underneath each category was space for type of shot and date given. I filled up two shot records before the age of eighteen.

What easier way to give a bunch of kid's shots than to just go to their school? We were not given a choice. Everyone was lined up and given the shot, or shots, of the day. Yes, sometimes we were given shots in both arms. The nurses were kind, but swamped. I certainly would not want to spend my day giving shots to a bunch of screaming kids. OK, not everyone screamed, but some sure did. Once, as I was moving out after having my shots, I came face-to-face with a First grader who was crying. She hadn't even had her shots yet. Thinking that I would be nice and reassure her that it wasn't that bad, I leaned down and said, "Don't worry. It only hurts a little." She took a good look at me and started really screaming. Seems that the good nurse had nicked a vein in my arm and blood was dripping off my fingertips. So much for good deeds.

Shortly after we moved to Area 2, I was asked to join the Girl Scouts, which I eagerly did. I had been disappointed when Mama would not let me join the 4-H Club in Portia. All my friends joined, and I was left out. Even though she explained to me that we were leaving soon and I would not be able to participate, I was still disappointed. In retrospect, becoming a Girl Scout was one of the best things I would do in my life.

Never will I forget my friend Lucinda Willis grabbing my hand and running with me across the school yard to attend my first Brownie meeting. I was so excited! Of course, there was a catch. The troop was so big that they could not add another girl without adding another leader. So, who did they ask? My mama, of course. She accepted, reluctantly. Mama was not a joiner. But she knew how much I wanted to belong, so she came to the meetings and did her part and I got to be a Girl Scout.

I loved everything about it. Even though it was late in the year, I got a Brownie uniform which I proudly wore to school along with my fellow Brownies on meeting day. As the school year was ending, it was time for the Brownies to fly up to Intermediate Girl Scouts. These were fourth through sixth graders. At the Fly-up ceremony, the leader who presented us with our Girl Scout pins asked each of us a question about the flag or our US government, which the troop had addressed before I joined. My question was, "How many stripes are there on the American flag?" I did not have a clue. Bless that woman's heart, she whispered the answer to me, 13, so I could answer so everyone could hear me give the answer. But I was still super embarrassed.

That summer, and many other summers, there was Day Camp. We met at the community center where we had our regular meetings. Most of the day was spent outside where we did all sorts of things, like learn how to tie knots and weave sit-upons out of newspaper. We even did some folk dancing. We took our lunch so we stayed most of the day. Too bad camp only lasted a week because it was fun.

When school started back in September. so did our regular meetings. Since we were now Intermediates, we could work on earning badges, not only at the meetings, but on our own at home. One of the first badges we earned was the Sewing badge so we could sew the badges we earned and other insignia on our uniforms. In our meetings, we not only worked on badges, but learned Girl Scout songs, how to tie yet more knots, the square knot being the most important, sing Grace, since the Girl Scouts never put a bite in their mouths without first singing Grace, how to boil an egg, and how a proper meeting is conducted. I learned patriotism, loyalty, respect for others, and leadership.

The Intermediate uniform was vastly different from the Brownie uniform. It was a green collared dress with long sleeves that buttoned all the way down the front. There was a thin green leather belt around the waist. Above the pocket on the right, we pinned our Girl Scout pin and the World Pin. The troop numbers went on the top of one sleeve and the badges we earned were sewn on the other sleeve, moving up the arm from the cuff. This was all topped off with a green felt beret.

That green felt beret would cause me a problem. The girls of our troop proudly wore our uniforms to school on meeting day. After all, we lived in a culture where uniforms were worn every day by our fathers. The Boy Scouts wore their uniforms on their meeting day. Our maids wore a uniform. My mother wore a uniform once a week when she volunteered as a Grey Lady. Uniforms were the norm.

I always came home for lunch since there was no cafeteria at school. Occasionally, Daddy was there for lunch, too. On this day, after we sat down to eat and before he said the blessing, Daddy said,

"Carolyn, take off your hat while you're at the table."

I said, "No."

Again, he asked me to remove my hat.

This time I said, "No. Ladies do not have to take their hats off in the house."

He replied, "But this is not the same. It is part of your uniform and YOU HAVE TO TAKE IT OFF!"

Again, I said, "No."

You know how it is not a good idea to rile up someone who is slow to anger? My dear daddy rarely showed any anger, but this time I crossed the line. He jumped up out of his chair, snatched that beret off my head, jerked me out of my chair and gave me a spanking I'll never forget. I screamed and cried. Daddy had never spanked me before. It was not that I had never been spanked. Mama was not averse to wielding a switch or her bare hand when she thought it was called for. But my Daddy. Oh, Lord!

Daddy grabbed his own hat and stormed out of the house. Mama and the maid peeked out of the kitchen where Mama had taken refuge sometime during my exchange with Daddy. I was sent to my room to calm down. Later, Mama came in with some advice. "Maybe you should have done what Daddy asked." She had a washcloth to wipe my face before I had to go back to school. I really do not remember the aftermath that evening but I do know that thereafter I took my hat off at the table because, I had learned, hats that were part of a uniform, even a Girl Scout uniform, were taken off in the house.

Army Brats do not have much "sameness" in their lives. They do not grow up in the same house in the same town going to the same school with the same friends. They do not frequent the same stores nor attend the same church. The only "sameness" in their lives is that, from time to time, everything changes. Their father is transferred and they move—different house, different school, different friends, sometimes even a different culture. They learn to wipe the dust off their feet and move on.

For me, two things remained the same---my parents and Girl Scouts. My parents were always there for me and no matter where we moved, there was always a Girl Scout troop on every post for me to join. These were girls who "spoke the same language," believed in the same values, sang the same songs, made the same promise, and believed in the same laws. It was a constant sisterhood during change. The Army, in its wisdom, always promoted Scouts. I guess the Army thought it kept the Brats in line, although it did not necessarily always work. Army Brats can be a rowdy bunch.

We may have lived behind a tall wire fence with MPs guarding the gate but that did not mean we stayed behind the fence. For one thing, there was the shopping center down Avenue D. It was just a short walk away. Of all the things that were there, the library was my favorite. I loved to read, and I loved the librarian. She was always directing me to good books. One of the books she directed me to was "Sister Carrie." I do not remember the story but what I got out of the book was my nickname. I wanted to be Carrie, too. So, I started to ask my friends to call me Carrie, which they did. Mama and Daddy were not really on board, but they tolerated the change. I was known as Carrie until I married. Sometimes, when I visited the library, I would curl up on the couch in the corner and read myself to sleep. The librarian would have to wake me up and send me home.

The second-best part of the shopping center was the movie theater. On Saturday mornings, for a dime, not a real dime, but a paper script dime, they showed serials — cowboys and Indians like Roy Rogers and Gene Autry. There were also silly comedies like Bud Abbott and Lou Costello. Me and my friends came prepared for the wild west. We always wore our six-shooter cap pistols on our hips and they were fully loaded. And they were always confiscated by the teenaged Japanese boys who worked at the theater. We picked then up on the way out and usually had a running gun battle all the way home.

The way home took us up the hill and through the parking lot of the chapel. Behind the chapel was a small Japanese cemetery. There were maybe twenty tall, skinny gravestones engraved with Japanese writing, usually with offerings in front of them. Dire things would happen to us if we messed with the gravestones or the offerings, so we left them alone. This little cemetery was probably much like the cemetery that we think got bulldozed off our hill that yielded the dead plate.

One Saturday night I went to see the latest movie, "The Thing." It was dark when we came out of the theater. The friends I was with all lived in Area 1, so we parted ways and I took the path up the hill by myself. That movie was super scary! The closer I got to the cemetery, the more I just knew something was going to be hiding behind one of those gravestones. I ran like a scared rabbit through the cemetery and all the way home. When I got home, I was afraid to go into my dark room without reaching around the door frame to switch on the light. It was many weeks before I could bring myself to go into my room without reaching to switch on the light lest a monster be waiting for me.

Best Toys Easter was not too far, plus the food carts and other Japanese businesses. But off the beaten path a little way was Sankeien Gardens. We called it Sunken Gardens. What it is, and I guess, was, is a sanctuary for historic buildings, or maybe iconic buildings from Japan's past. I do not remember the buildings. I think they were behind a tall fence that we were not interested in scaling. There were extensive gardens, a statue of the Goddess of Mercy, and big pools of water lilies. That is why we called the place Sunken Gardens, because there was what we thought was quicksand in the pools of water where the water lilies grew. Who found that out, I do not know. That knowledge was just passed down from kid to kid. The newbies found out about the quicksand when old hands would persuade the newbies to jump in the water lily ponds. They sank up to their waist, if not a little deeper! Then they would get pulled out and charged with keeping the secret until the next new kid came along.

Going back and forth on our adventures, we often wandered into the Japanese neighborhoods. No one cared. You would think that the adults would have been just a little concerned that their kids were wandering around places where our recently conquered enemies lived. Not so. We already had seen that the Japanese love their kids and tolerate their high-jinks up to a certain age. Of course, after they get to that certain age, they do have to toe the line. I guess the Japanese just extended that tolerance to the wandering American kids.

Now, we did not live in an American bubble. Mama and Daddy sampled the Japanese culture often and mostly took me with them on their outings. One day we were just riding around in a Japanese neighborhood when suddenly Mama yelled, "Charles, look! Oh! Carolyn, don't look!" I poked my nosy head over the back of the front seat and there, strolling across the street in front of the car was a naked Japanese woman. No one was batting an eye except we Americans. She seemed to be going from one bathhouse to another, and in no hurry to do so. We moved on, as did she. Things were different in Japan.

Even though we lived in Japan and had close contact with the Japanese, we did not learn to speak their language. We did learn how to be polite, though. And being polite is very important to the Japanese. We learned how to properly bow, hands together in front, eyes down. And how to say polite things. Here is a list of polite things I learned to say:

- Good morning—Ohayo   Good day or good afternoon---Konnichi-wa
- Good evening---Konban-wa   Good night---Oyasumi
- How are you? --Ikaga desu ka?   Thank you---Arigato
- You're welcome---Doitashimashita Please---Dozo
- Good-by---Sayonara   Yes---Hai   No---Iie

Daddy always called me his ichi-ban corbito---Number one sweetheart. And I learned to count. I can count to twenty, probably more if I put my mind to it.

We went to the theater, too. I saw my first opera, a performance of "Madam Butterfly," which I loved. This was certainly not The Rockettes in New York city. Then we went to a Kabuki theatre performance. That was different! There was no proscenium arch, no curtain, the musicians were seated on the stage playing traditional Japanese instruments and the set and costumes were changed on stage by stagehands dressed all in black. Even their faces were covered in black masks. The performance went on as the changes were made. Nobody missed a beat. I see that now in current theatre performances. Then it was novel. I am guessing that's something else we imported from Japan.

Sometimes we would pack a picnic lunch and go down to Kamakura where the statue of the Great Buddha was. He was huge! Made of metal sitting on a dais with legs crossed. Years later, when I went back for a visit, I expected that he would not look as big as I remembered him because usually things observed in childhood turn out not as big as you remember. Not so in this case. He was bigger, much bigger! I had even forgotten that you could go inside him and that there was a window in the back of his head. The Buddhists were there to worship him. They left offerings at his feet, clapping their hands before they offered their prayers so he would be sure to hear them. Mama said not to look. How would we like it if someone stared at us as we said the Lord's Prayer?

On the grounds were picnic tables where we had our lunch. Once, when we were there, the Samurai warriors were there. They were demonstrating their warrior skills. They charged each other on their horses, wielding their swords in large arcs over their heads. There was combat on the ground, with swords but also with long pikes. And there were some physical contact battles, where they jumped and kicked and pivoted and sometimes threw each other to the ground. It was quite a show. Besides the Samurai warriors, there were Geisha girls walking around. They were so pretty in their flowery kimonos and oboes. I guess they were there to see the Samurai and to be seen by the ordinary people. Now,

Mama and I both had kimonos and oboes that Tsuda-san made for us, but we could not hold a candle to those girls.

One summer we went down to Kyoto. We had friends from Ft. Hamilton who lived there whom we wanted to visit. We toured Kyoto, a very important city in the history of Japan. I remember the tall walls of the Imperial Palace. There was a mote surrounding it with an impressive bridge over the mote. We could not go in because it was still a residence of Emperor Hirohito. There were geisha girls on the streets of Kyoto, too. We stayed at a lakeside hotel, which was nice, but not as nice as the Fuji View. One day we went fishing, or at least, Daddy went fishing. We rowed around the lake in a rowboat. Mama and I were just along for the ride, which, by the way, was neat. Daddy caught some fish and the hotel kitchen staff fixed them for our dinner that night. And they were good!

Occasionally, we would go into Tokyo. For one thing, the big PX was there. They had more and better stuff than our little PX in Yokohama. The PX was on the Ginza, which was Tokyo's answer to New York's Fifth Avenue. Mama and Daddy did some serious shopping while we were in Japan. They bought things that I am pretty sure they thought they would not be able to afford in the States, like full sets of China and silverware, plus some jewelry. Mama got a beautiful string of Mikimoto pearls with matching broach and earrings. There were a few other stores on the Ginza where Mama got in some shopping, too. On another note, rumor was that Mrs. General Wainwright made them close the PX when they got a new delivery of clothes so she could have first dibs. I believed it then but do not know that I do now, though general's wives did have some privileges the rest of the officers' wives did not. Whatever the case, they were certainly often in the rumor mill.

Once, after church on Sunday, we went to the Imperial Hotel in Tokyo for Sunday dinner. The Imperial Hotel was designed by Frank Lloyd Wright. It was said to have a special foundation that would swing back and forth during an earthquake so the building would not crumble. As we were coming in, guess who was going out? General McArthur! He was the Supreme Commander! No one was more important in our lives than Gen. McArthur. Daddy snapped to attention, gave him a sharp salute, and said, "Good afternoon, General." McArthur gave him a sloppy salute back and said, "Afternoon, son. Have a nice dinner." Then he and his entourage moved on. He spoke to us! We were so thrilled!

I remember when General McArthur was dismissed by President Truman. Daddy was then stationed at Haneda Airport, so he was there when the MacArthur's came to board their plane back to the States. The Japanese came out in droves to say good-by. There were hundreds of people there, waving American flags, shouting their approval of his handling of the Occupation, sorry to see him go, especially under the circumstances. He had to be pleased, probably mentally thumbing his nose at President Truman.

One day, as we walked down the steps to school, we noticed something different. All up and down Avenue D, the Japanese flag was flying. We had never seen that before. The Japanese were forbidden to display their flag. They were a conquered, occupied country. But now the Occupation was over. It was over on September 8, 1951, but did not go into effect until April 28, 1952. Things would begin to change for the Japanese people. Restrictions would be lifted; life would be easier. The Americans would go home.

And go home we did. Not all of us. There is still an American Army and Navy presence in Japan, but now it is at the invitation of the Japanese government. The Hornbuckle's packed up and left on August 23, 1952. I was eight years old when we arrived and was now eleven. Not a lifetime, by any means, but a good chunk of childhood.

We may have come with only our clothes, but we left with a whole lot more. Some furniture, pictures, China, lamps, figurines, and wonderful memories that have lasted a lifetime. Daddy sold the car—Betsy—to an Australian officer wearing one of those neat turned up hats. We gave the cat away with unknown results, said our good-byes and got on a Flying Tiger plane headed East. On the way over the Pacific, we landed on Wake Island to refuel. The pilot invited all the kids on board to stand in the cockpit and look out the windshield. I happened to be up there as we approached Wake Island, so I got a good look at the island. It is shaped like a sloppy V with a lagoon in the middle. I could not stay while the plane landed, but the view was awesome. Later in the flight we landed in Honolulu, also to refuel. We were not allowed to get off the plane, darn it.

Sometime during the flight, when everyone was asleep, the plane hit an air pocket and suddenly lost elevation. It was like we fell in a big, deep hole. That was scary. The pilot assured us that everything was OK and we continued. We landed in San Francisco, then boarded another plane for Oklahoma City. In Oklahoma City we changed planes for Little Rock where the family would meet us. In the Oklahoma City airport, it was accidently pointed out to me how long I had lived in Occupied Japan. I wanted a candy bar, so Mama gave me a fistful of change. At the concession stand, I picked out a Hershey bar. The lady said, "That will be a quarter." Suddenly, I was bumfuzzled. I did not know which one was the quarter! We had always had military script, paper nickels, dimes, and quarters, instead of actual coins. I just held out my hand and said, "Which one is the quarter!" She took the quarter and looked at me like I was crazy. What kid does not know what a quarter looks like? The kid who just spent the last thirty-two months in Japan, that is who.

Carolyn Green

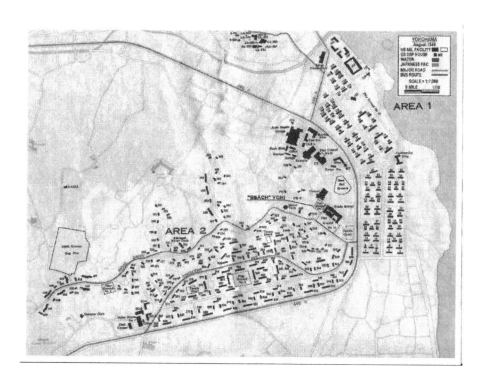

124

P B & ?

Well, we were Stateside. We had left Japan, but life in Occupied Japan would never leave us. Not only did we have physical reminders---lamps, tables, pictures, plates, etc., but we had memories. It had been a good life. Things had gone mostly well. We had experienced another culture. We had learned that our way wasn't the only way and that was OK. We would appreciate what we had, not just physical things but our country and how it worked and how important loyalty to our country was. I don't think we, any of us, ever expressed those feelings out loud, but they were there. From then on, we were set apart from most of the people we knew because of where we had lived and what we had experienced.

Certainly, we were not the only people to live in Occupied Japan, nor, for that matter, to live in an occupied country. There were also plenty of people who lived in occupied countries in Europe. But our experiences were unique. We belonged to a little tribe of folks who didn't quite fit the norm.

When we arrived in the States, we went first to Portia, Arkansas to Mama's family. Then we went to Poplar Bluff, Missouri to Daddy's parents. Daddy had thirty days leave before he had to report to his new station in Fort Leonard Wood, Missouri. We spent the time catching up with everyone, telling tales, hearing tales, and just enjoying each other's company. It had been a long time.

When Daddy's thirty days were over, he went off to Ft. Wood and, no surprise here, Mama and I had to stay in Poplar Bluff because there were no quarters available on post. We would come later when something opened up. Meanwhile, we moved into my parents' house at 225 N. 10th Street. It had been rented out all the time we were gone. I guess our furniture had been in storage somewhere. It was delivered and we moved in.

This was really not much of a house. It had one bedroom, one bathroom, a kitchen, living room and dining room. There was also front and back porches and a full basement. It was small. It sat at the top of a hill on a small rise above the street. There was a retaining wall and five or six steps up to the narrow front yard and then a sidewalk leading up to the front porch steps. The car, when we had one, was parked beside the house on a gravel driveway. It had been fine for Mama and Daddy before I came along. Now, Mama's bed was in the dining room and I occupied the bedroom. We ate at a small table in the kitchen. The only thing big about 225 N. 10th St. was the backyard. It was flat and went back forever. Well, at least a long way. There were no trees on the property, only grass. The neighbor's vegetable garden backed up to the back of our lot.

There was a pretty steep retaining wall bordering our lot and the house next door on the downside of the hill. You didn't want to go over the edge. I know this from experience. The one feature in the backyard was a big white smooth rock sticking out of the ground in the middle of the yard. It must have been at least three feet tall. Daddy said he tried to dig it out when they bought the house and no matter how far down he went, it just kept keeping on. So, there it was and there it stayed. Sometimes it served as third base, sometimes a hill if we were playing King of the Hill except it was slick and pointy and no one could really stand on it. Most of the time it was just in the way.

We didn't have a car. Daddy had the car. I don't remember what kind of car it was, but my best guess would be an Oldsmobile and that it was red. Pretty sure her name was Betsy since all our cars were named Betsy. Betsy spent the week at Ft. Wood and brought Daddy to Poplar Bluff most weekends. During the week, Mama had to make do. Since both grandparents had vehicles, I am guessing that one of them gave her a ride when she needed it or that her friends picked her up for bridge games or shopping. There was a neighborhood grocery store several blocks away and it was usually, ok, always, my job to run to the grocery store for milk or bread or whatever we were out of. One time I was playing hopscotch and dropped a quart jar of milk on the sidewalk. Of course, it broke and spattered glass all over the sidewalk. I cried all the way home because I knew I would be in big trouble. Actually, I wasn't. Mama went with me to the site of the disaster and helped me clean it up and then walked with me back to the store to get another quart of milk which she probably carried home. Life is easier with a car.

We also got to know our neighbors. The corner lot was empty and the people down the hill were not too sociable. But behind us lived the Bennetts. They were an older couple, empty nesters, but their son did live in town. Boss Bennett was President of the Bank of Poplar Bluff. Mrs. Bennett was a really nice lady, especially since she forgave me when I accidently burned up her garden. I was burning leaves in the back yard and let the fire get away from me. Since it was Fall, most everything growing in the garden was finished producing. Still, it's not a good idea to burn your neighbor's veggies. Mama was really mad and embarrassed.

But the Bennetts were kind. They had a TV set. This was still the time when there weren't too many TVs in the homes. For one thing, there weren't very many TV stations. The only one close enough to Poplar Bluff was the station in Cape Girardeau, and in those days, they weren't broadcasting 24/7 like they do now. Midnight came and they were off the air until five or six in the morning. But on Sunday nights we were always invited to come watch Ed Sullivan's variety show and Gunsmoke. That was neat.

Part of living in Poplar Bluff was that we were close to my Hornbuckle grandparents. They lived south of town on a few acres. There was a large garden, a hen house, a detached garage, and several rows of grapes, plus the house. Granddaddy puttered in the garage, he was a mechanic, and hunted quail and squirrels in the fields surrounding the house. What always drove my mama crazy was that when Granddaddy brought his kill home, he always just left it on a bench on the back porch. It was Grandmother's job to get it ready to cook. Mama always thought that if he killed it, he ought to clean it. That wasn't going to happen. Grandmother tended the garden and canned whatever extra came out of the garden. She also made jelly from the blackberry bushes on the property and did a little sewing.

I got to participate in all the things they did to occupy their time. This was something new for me since I had never lived close to them except when I was a baby. I learned how to use Granddaddy's big clamp that was attached to his worktable. I clamped old wire and pipes and then bent them into different shapes. I learned how to hammer without hitting my fingers, the names of the screw heads and how to screw things together. Basically,

I was being the grandson he would never have. He took me hunting one time. Given my reaction to killing something, that was enough for both of us. But I learned how to shoot a gun and could mostly hit an old can balanced on a fence post. Somehow, I don't think he was very impressed with his substitute grandson. He would much rather have had the real thing.

Grandmother Hornbuckle took me to the garden to harvest whatever was ready. She also took me to pick blackberries. They mostly grew along the fence row along the road. We picked the berries and the chiggers picked us. Ugh! Sometimes I wondered if it was worth it. But I really do like blackberry jelly. She really didn't want me cooking or canning with her. I think she thought I was mostly in the way, which was probably right. She did let me carry the newly canned jars down to the basement where they were lined up on shelves along one wall. She clearly canned much more than they could eat. I also got to go with her to gather eggs. This was not new, since my other grandmother beat her to that experience before we left for Japan. I could gather eggs, but her old rooster was another story. He was mean. He would attack if you didn't watch out. Not my favorite chicken, I learned to never let him get between me and the gate so I could make a quick getaway if necessary, and it most always was.

We also harvested grapes. There was grape jelly but if those grapes were turned into something else, I don't remember it. Grandmother was a staunch teetotaler. Granddaddy had been a heavy drinker in his younger days, but those days were over. There must have been some alcohol in the house because at Christmas grandmother always made two fruitcakes, one with, and one without, booze. The boozy one was really boozy, but she didn't know it because she never tasted it. Don't ask me how I knew about that boozy cake. Ha!

Somewhere along the way, I came to understand that my grandparents, particularly my grandmother, didn't really like me. They tolerated me, but I wasn't the grandson they wanted. I was not going to carry on the Hornbuckle name. Nothing was ever said, but I knew. Both grandparents had difficult childhoods and I think it colored their adult take on life, making both of them difficult people to please. After all, this was the mother who threatened to shoot her twenty-year-old daughter with a shotgun if she left the house to go to a party on a weeknight. This was the father who beat his son with a strop strap on his tenth birthday because he was teasing his father about getting a spanking for his birthday. Interestingly, my mama didn't know that I knew until I was an adult. I just thought it was a given.

September came and I had to go to school. Daddy was really pleased that I was going to attend the same school he went to as a kid. Kenyon school was within walking distance of our house. The school hadn't changed much since Daddy went there except for the fire escape. In his day, it was a large metal tube that went from the third floor to the ground. During a fire drill, the kids were expected to sit in it and slide down to safety. Daddy said that you didn't want to be the first kid down because the tube was filled with spiderwebs. I was glad it was gone.

My teacher asked me to share my experiences in Japan. To that end, one day I wore my kimono and obie to school. I showed my classmates my clothes and how they were worn. I counted to ten in Japanese and taught them how to say please and thank you in Japanese. They were impressed, I think. But it set me apart and that was not what I wanted. I wanted to be part of the crowd. But I did make friends and was included in the out-of-school activities, like birthday parties and going to the show on Saturday afternoon. And, of course, I joined a Girl Scout troop. That saved the day, as it always would. But I was always that girl who was different, who had lived in Japan.

I really don't remember how long it was before we moved to Ft. Wood. I was anxious to get back to Army life, to a culture that I understood, to be the regular kid, not one who stood out. Fort Leonard Wood offered all that, and more. Or so I hoped.

INSERT PICTURE

INTO THE WOOD

Our brief sojourn in Poplar Bluff was over. Quarters became available and Mama and I moved to Fort Leonard Wood. Ft. Wood is in the middle of nowhere, at the northernmost reaches of the Ozarks Plateau. When we got there, it had been around for about fifteen years. It was principally a training camp. It was huge, covering many square acres of woods and streams. Over the years, it saw a lot of soldiers come and go. That was Daddy's job, to see that the soldiers both came and went when and where they were supposed to.

What was then Route 66 passed by the access road that went through the woods to the Main Gate. There was a small sign pointing the way, and that was it. It was low profile to the public. Of course, the fort was surrounded by high fences. Entrances and exits were controlled by MPs manning the gates. Just because someone wanted in didn't mean they got in. The proper sticker had to be on the car and, if asked, the proper ID had to be produced. I guess you could say we lived in a gated community.

Straight ahead through the front gate, and down another road through the woods, was the main area of the fort which featured the Headquarters Building and the various offices needed to run the fort. Also, the barracks area for the soldiers was nearby. This was the heart of the operation.

When you came through the front gate and turned right up a hill and drove through more woods, you came to the housing area for the officers' dependents. This was where we lived, on Rolla Street. Most of the housing was not stand-alone houses, but barracks-like buildings divided into four apartments. We lived in one of the end units. Each unit consisted of three bedrooms and one bathroom upstairs. Downstairs there was an eat-in kitchen, a living room, and a furnace room just inside the back door which faced the street. The front door in the living room opened out on a tiny yard backed up by the woods. We brought our own furniture. Cars were parked on the street.

Up the street, within walking distance, was the commercial area, basically "downtown." This consisted of a PX with a little café, a commissary, a movie theater, a community building, a playground, and tennis courts. There was a pool, but it was at the Officers' Club. The only thing missing was a chapel. On Sunday mornings, church was in the movie theater.

But, yes, there was something else missing, a school. There was no school on post. We were bussed into Waynesville, the nearest town with a school. Waynesville was the county seat of Pulaski County. What was then the "main drag" of the entire country, Route 66, went right by the town. Out by Route 66 there were multiple gas stations, motels, and cafes to attract all the cars going by. Otherwise, it was a sleepy farm town with the county courthouse in the center of the square. What the townsfolk felt they did not need were hundreds of Army Brats filling up their schools to overflowing. Too bad, because there we were. It didn't take long for even a sixth grader to understand that WE WERE NOT WELCOME, not in town and not in the schools.

We were told that at some point the Army decided to address that issue. One month, everyone on post was paid in cash, not just cash, but in two-dollar bills kind of cash. The idea was that the locals would change their minds when the $2.00 bills started showing up in droves in their cash registers. Clever. Money does talk.

My sixth-grade class was housed in the high school building because the elementary school was full. We were the only grade school class in the building. We heard the high school kids coming and going in the hall outside our door. We were told, above all else, to stay out of their way. I imagine they were also told to stay out of our way. It made for an interesting set-up.

I'm pretty sure that my teacher, Mrs. McAlpine, would much rather have had only the local kids in her classroom than the Army Brats. Hey, we were in the minority. Unlike the locals, whose idea of a big trip was going down the road to Springfield, we Army Brats had been all over the world and were not much impressed with Ozarks culture. We greeted each other in German, French, or Japanese, and, yes, we were showing off. We laughed at the girl who could yodel. Really, she was quite good at it, but we would never let her know we thought that. The two cultures just didn't quite jive.

Some good things did happen to me in the sixth grade. For one thing, I got a boyfriend, my first. His name was Rocky Crooks. He, too, was an Army Brat. He was a tall redhead who lived across the street. Also, for some reason, the sixth graders were included in either the Homecoming or Prom festivities. I don't remember which one. Maybe because of the location of our classroom, the high schoolers couldn't leave us out. Anyway, I was chosen to represent my class which meant I had to have a formal dress. My classmate/escort had to have suit. We were really going to be dressed up! Mama and I went to Springfield to shop and I chose a pretty pink formal with tulle over the skirt and shoulders. We were presented as part of the Court at the dance. Problem was, my escort couldn't dance very well, and neither could I. Oh, well, at least we got fancy clothes.

Right away, I joined the Girl Scout troop. There it was, that sameness that I loved. My fellow scouts didn't disappoint. We made the same pledge, believed in the same laws, and sang the same songs. This time, we didn't wear our uniforms to school. We met at the community center, worked on badges, and did some camping. At Ft. Wood there was a Scout hut on the bank of one of the streams. We had to share it with the Boy Scouts, but that was okay. There was a fire pit where we could roast marshmallows and hot dogs over the flames. If we stayed the night, we put our sleeping bags down on the floor inside the hut. No mosquitoes, which was a good thing. Just being in the woods of the beautiful Ozarks was a good thing.

Our leader was a young Army wife who had been a Girl Scout growing up so she knew the drill. For a while, she and her husband lived on the other end of our building. Once, a few of us in the troop were visiting her house. I don't remember why she wasn't around. She may have been upstairs looking for something. Meanwhile, we were looking for something to do, or maybe snooping around and found, in the back of a bookcase, her husband's stash of dirty comic books. That was quite a revelation. I didn't know such things existed. Suffice it to say, we got a quick education in, what should I say?, forbidden literature. Not any knowledge we could use to earn a badge. We stashed them away when we heard her coming and never told a soul. Our little secret.

Seventh grade was no big deal except that we were now in the brand- new Junior High building. My teacher was an Army wife. She was nice but didn't take any gruff from the army brats. She had a couple of her own at home. As seventh graders, we were offered the opportunity to join the band. We would be taught to play an instrument. I chose the clarinet. One thing I am not is musical. Mama always wanted me to be. In Brooklyn, I had taken piano lessons. I was never any good and didn't like it much. I guess I yielded to Mama's urging, so gave music another try. It was fun being in the band but I was never going to stand out, at least not in a good way. One time we went to Springfield for a band competition and did so bad that our director stopped us in the middle of our piece and made us start over. Suffice it to say that we didn't win any awards.

I did learn one thing from being in the band, though. After that bus trip to Springfield, when we got back to Waynesville, we had to find a way home. One of my friend's mothers was going to give me a ride, but one of the upper- class boys, a trumpet player, asked if he could take me home. I said yes. He was pretty hot and was definitely a good catch. A bunch of kids climbed in his car. He dropped them all off in town and then it was just us. Instead of getting on the highway, he headed down a dirt road under a bridge over Route 66 to a spot on the river, a make-out spot. This was all new to me. I didn't really know what to expect. His advances scared me to death. I realized that I was very vulnerable out in the middle of nowhere. I pushed him away a couple of times and asked to go home. I guess he thought I would be more willing, but he relented and silently took me home. I couldn't get out of that car fast enough. We avoided each other after that. Lesson learned. Over the years, I have driven over the bridge past that spot many times and I always remember that night and how scared I was.

These were transition years. I went from a pretty decent little girl to a horrible teenager. The day I turned thirteen, even though I'm pretty sure my parents didn't, I celebrated. Now I could join the Teen Club! I could go to the dances. I could listen to rock and roll. (Daddy hated it.) I could have a date. I could go out at night. I did have a curfew, though. I could, and did, make out with my boyfriend on the back row at the picture show on Saturday night. (And then attend Sunday School and church on the front row of the same theater on Sunday morning.) Mama always said that she never knew when I came downstairs in the morning if I was going to be five, or thirteen or thirty that day. Suffice it to say that I tried out several iterations of maturity.

Maturity wasn't always in the forefront. One night my friends and I had gone to the movies. We were making our way home. As we passed the tennis courts, we decided to have a little fun. We tore the nets off their stakes and wrapped them around a small outbuilding adjacent to the courts. That act of vandalism was never pinned on us, thank heavens. There were too many other candidates.

One thing that maturity brought was an awareness of different personalities, good and bad. At that age, I probably could not put into words what I was learning, but the awareness was somewhat there. Case in point, my girlfriend up the street had two pet rabbits. She and her little brother loved those rabbits. Any time I was there, we played with the rabbits. One day I was walking by their house and saw them sitting at the table in the kitchen. Everyone's kitchen table was by the front window, so we always waved at whoever was sitting there. Not this time. I could see that she and her brother were crying. What on earth was wrong?

As soon as I could, I called her to find out what was going on. It wasn't good. Her Dad had decided that he had had enough of the rabbits, so he killed them, and made my friend and her brother watch while he skinned them and cut them up. Then he forced his wife to cook them for dinner. What I saw was them being forced to eat their pet rabbits. "Take a bite, chew it up and swallow it.," their daddy demanded. How does someone get to be so cruel?

In retrospect, I think that there are two types of personalities that are drawn to the military. One type is the one who values aggression. Get out there. Lead with force. Make the enemy sorry they ever engaged you. I guess that's okay when you are leading troops, but not when you bring it home to your family. Looking back, I saw that attitude play out several times in my childhood. My friend Lucinda had to leave Yokohama early because her father beat up her mother. Our neighbor in Area 2, the MP officer, physically threw his son out of the house during a fight over some clothes left on the floor. There would be a few more examples in my future.

The other personality is the one who values structure and order. Rules. Everything is predictable. Everything has a place. That was my dad. He didn't have to decide what to wear to work. He wore his uniform. He didn't have to think how to respond to a request. He said, "Yes, Sir." And did it. His rank told him and everyone else what his duties and expectations were and how he would be treated and treat everyone else. You did what you were ordered to do and didn't question that order. Sometimes my dad did question and that got him in trouble with some of his superior officers. But when that personality brings it home, it's much easier to live with.

On a lighter note, one of the things I found hard to live with was the whip-or-will who lived in the tree outside my bedroom window. They're nice birds except when they whip-or-will repeatedly all night, loudly. When he started up, I would yell at him to go away. He did, but he came right back. Closing the window didn't really help. That was his tree, not mine, and if he wanted to sit there and scream all night, he was going to do it. If I could have reached the tree, I would have given it a good shake, but I couldn't reach it. Actually, if I could have reached it, I probably would have used it as an escape route to sneak out of the house at night. I knew one kid who regularly climbed out of his house that way. As it was, I couldn't sneak out at all because the stairs squeaked too loud. Probably not a bad thing in the long run.

Another thing I decided to do was to keep a diary. I read a lot of Nancy Drew books and I think she kept a diary. Anyway, I went to the PX and picked out a nice one with a lock on it. This was to be private, no Mama looking at what I would write. I hid the key so she couldn't cheat. I wrote every night for six or seven months, then it got old and I slacked off until I finally quit altogether. A couple of years later, probably during yet another move, I found it stuck at the bottom of a drawer. When I opened it to read my seventh-grade history, to my surprise, every one of the entries began, "Dear Dairy." I was so embarrassed. I threw it away.

Since coming back to the States, we now had no maid to cook and clean. In Poplar Bluff, I had pitched in a little bit, but now that I was a teenager, I was expected to really get busy and help with the housework. I had to make my bed, change the sheets, dust, and run the vacuum sweeper. Not always, but some of the time. Also, I had to learn how to iron. Mama started me off with ironing the pillowcases and Daddy's handkerchiefs. Later I graduated to sheets and shirts. I also had to set the table, and do it right. Washing the dishes was something that Mama and Daddy always did together. Daddy washed and Mama dried and put the dishes up. Sometimes I dried, but not often. That was their time.

Of course, we had a cat. This one came from the lady who had been my Sunday School teacher in Yokohama.

Her husband was transferred to someplace where they couldn't take the cat, so she gave me the cat. She was absolutely beautiful! A long-haired pure white Persian whose name I can't remember. She had beautiful green eyes, liked to snuggle, and shed her hair all over the house. (Maybe why I had to run the sweeper.) There was no potty box. She went outside to do her business.

One night she was out, and we heard a screech and a yowl. We rushed out to see what was going on. No one was there but the cat. She had clearly been attacked by some wild animal or another dog or cat. She had a scratch on her ear and a wound on her side but was no worse for the wear, or so we thought. We were wrong. In a few days, she was clearly sick. A trip to the vet brought bad news. She most likely had rabies. In those days, the only sure way to tell was a postmortem blood sample. She couldn't be put to sleep. She had to stay at the vet's until she died, then her head and a blood sample would be sent to Jefferson City for a final test. This was awful news. We were all devastated.

We said good-by at the vet's office and went home to await the news that she had died and the samples had been sent off. Time was of the essence, because, a couple of days after the attack, I had a birthday party. There were lots of girls in the house, and of course, the cat came to the party. She was not one to miss out on being petted and admired. One of the girls who was at the party had a scratch on her arm that she couldn't account for. She didn't remember the cat scratching her, but she had held the cat and couldn't be certain she wasn't scratched. The reason this was important was because the blood test confirmed that the cat did indeed have rabies and everyone in contact with her had to have the rabies shots. That meant for the next fourteen days, me, Mama, Daddy, and my girlfriend had to go to the hospital and get a shot. No one wants rabies, but getting fourteen shots was not high on the list either, especially when the boys at school found out and made it a point to punch us in the arm. It was a while before we had another cat.

True to form, my daddy wanted me to know what it was that he did. As he had taken me to the Port of Yokohama to see what was going on, now he would take me with him when he had to go to Vichy to the airport. Fort Wood didn't have an airport, so they used the airport at Vichy, a really small town just north of the fort. We would go there in the evening or on Saturday so Daddy could check flights coming and going. The runway was short, so it couldn't accommodate large planes. Whatever came and went had to be cargo, not troops. I did get to go up in the flight tower and get a full view of the whole airport. That was neat. Neater still was that my daddy wanted to share what he did with me. Not every daddy does that.

Our time at Fort Wood was short, less than two years for Mama and me. Daddy was to be transferred to Narsarwack Air Force base in Greenland. And there was a catch. The school on post only went through the eighth grade. If dependents accompanied the officer, his tour was two years. It was one year if he went alone. Well, I was about to be an eighth grader. If we went to Greenland, where would I go to school for the ninth grade? There were a few options. The one I really wanted was to go to Germany to the Army Brats boarding school there. Evidently, my parents never considered that a real option. Rats!

I could come back to the States and live with my Uncle Fred and Aunt Vada in Portia where the Junior High in neighboring Black Rock was the pits. Or, I could go to Poplar Bluff and live with my Grandmother and Granddaddy Hornbuckle and attend Poplar Bluff Junior High. That wasn't really an option since my grandparents were not my biggest fans. They would probably have killed me. The only other option was to bite the bullet, say good-by to Daddy for a full year and Mama and I move back to Poplar Bluff where I would go to eighth grade in the same building where Daddy went to High School. When Daddy came home, we would move to wherever he was assigned. And that's what we did. Good-by, Fort Leonard Wood.

POPLAR BLUFF—AGAIN

Once again, we were moving. This move wasn't different, and where we were going wasn't different, because we were going back to Poplar Bluff. Through the years, when Mama and I couldn't go with Daddy, we went to Poplar Bluff. This time, I would be in the eighth grade.

A little history of our moves here, just to catch up. Mama and I moved from East Prairie to Poplar Bluff, to the little house they owned on North 10th Street when Daddy joined the Army. I was probably three years old. After he finished Basic Training and Officer Candidate School, we did a brief stint in Seattle, where I think he was in charge of an anti-aircraft gun on the coast. On our way to Seattle, on the train, I did what I always did if given the chance, I ran off. How do you run off on a train? You slip out of your compartment while your mother takes a nap. Then you make your way to the Lounge car. That's where my panicked mama found me, sitting on some kind soldier's lap, watching a game of poker. I guess that's when I became an official Army Brat.

Then it was back to Poplar Bluff briefly before we joined Daddy in Fort Eustis, Virginia where he went to the Transportation School. This was when we lived in Lee

Hall. After the T-school was finished, Mama and I went, once again, back to P.B. while Daddy went to Charleston, S.C. to be a transport commander. That meant that while he was on a Navy ship, he was in charge of everything that belonged to the Army. That meant the Army supplies that were being shipped to the battle zones and the troops who were on board destined for battle somewhere. He sailed multiple times out of Charleston as part of a large Navy fleet that zig-zagged across the Atlantic Ocean guarded by battle ships and submarines. He went to England, Europe, and the Mediterranean. He brought back lots of pretty things for Mama like Persian rugs, alabaster bowls, and an antique carriage clock. It so happened that he was in charge of the troop ship that brought the first War Brides from England to the States.

But I was not through running away. While Daddy was zigzagging back and forth across the Atlantic, Mama and I were living in Poplar Bluff. One day, Mama and I were downtown in the dime store. I saw a man in uniform at the back of the store. Daddy! I took off running as hard and as fast as I could, screaming at the top of my voice, "Daddy! Daddy!" When I got to him, I wrapped my arms around his legs, still screaming.

Well, it wasn't Daddy. It was some young soldier home on leave after finishing Basic Training. He certainly wasn't my father. Mama came running, disentangled me, and apologized all over the place. Both were pretty embarrassed. People who saw what happened would surely ask questions. Why did Elsie Jane's daughter think Billy Joe was her daddy? Is there something we don't know? My question was, why wasn't he my daddy? He had on a uniform. The sad truth is that I had not seen my father in so long that I had forgotten what he looked like. That is sad enough, but think of all the kids whose fathers never came home. I was one of the lucky ones.

When the war over, Daddy was stationed at Fort Hamilton, then the Port of New York. I dropped out of Kindergarten, and mama and I moved to Brooklyn, New York. When it was September, I started First Grade at P.S. 104, then we moved and I did most, but not quiet all, of the Second Grade at P.S. 102. After that, it was off to Japan with a short stop in Portia, Arkansas where we awaited travel orders. After Japan, Mama and I landed back in Poplar Bluff for a short time while we waited for quarters at Fort Leonard Wood. That assignment lasted two years. Now, Daddy was assigned to Greenland and we weren't going. Mama and I were going back to Poplar Bluff yet again.

There would be things that would be the same! We would be living in the same house, have the same neighbors, attend the same church, and, while it was the same school system, a different school, but just like sixth grade, the same building where my daddy went to school, only now it was the Junior High and not the Senior High School. Sameness was not something I was used to.

The best "same" was my friends. I would actually know some of the kids in my class this time. That was awesome! Never before had I started school and not been a total stranger. I caught up with my girlfriends and my Girl Scout troop, as well as a few of the boys, this time potential boyfriends.

Oh, there was another "same." The band teacher at Waynesville had taken the job as music teacher/band director at the Junior and Senior High Schools in Poplar Bluff. I signed up for band, and, while it was nice to have the same teacher, I soon dropped out. I just am not musical, so I opted to do us both a favor and put up my clarinet for good.

Of course, not everything was the same. Since this was Junior High, we changed classes. That was different, but okay. Classes included English, History, some kind of Math and some kind of science. There was Study Hall, but, if memory serves, no Art class and no Phys. Ed. Since the school buildings were so close to downtown, there was no room for a playing field. The High School had a basketball court, but that was all. The athletes were bussed to the football stadium/field house on the northwest edge of town for practice and games. Later the whole school complex moved out there.

As for classes, I liked English and History. Eighth grade history was Missouri History, which came in handy when I was expected to teach it to my seventh and eighth grade Special Ed students in St. James. (They could not have cared less.) Math and Science classes, not so much, mostly because I struggled with those subjects. Math was boring and definitely not my strong suite. Basically, I hated it.

But one particular math class stands out in my memory. The teacher, and I don't remember his name, was not doing anything to relieve the boredom. He droned on and on. One of the kids in the back of the room started throwing spitballs. Most of the other kids joined in the fun, tossing spitballs every time the teacher turned his back to the class to write on the blackboard. I, of course, was doing my part to insure no one was bored. I flung a particularly juicy spitball just as the teacher turned around to face the class. It hit him right smack in the cheek. All of a sudden, you could have heard a pin drop in that classroom. "Who threw that?" he asked as he wiped my spit off his face. Instead of looking at the floor as they should have, the whole class looked at me! Not only was I betrayed, I was busted, big time! The teacher was really angry and sent me directly to the principal's office. As you can imagine, I was scared to death.

The principal was a long-time educator. He had been around a long time. In his early days, he had been my daddy's coach in football, basketball, and track. The Hornbuckle name was not new to him. I'm sure also not new was some kid getting caught throwing spitballs in class.

I was ushered into his office and took a seat facing him. "Why are you here, Carolyn?," he asked. I told him that I had hit Mr. What's-his-name in the face with a spitball. "Did you mean to hit him?" "No, Sir. I've never hit anything I aimed at in my life." "Are you going to do it again?" "No, sir, never." I replied. "Ok," he said, as he leaned back in his chair. "Now, tell me about your dad. Where is he this time?" I filled him in on Daddy's whereabouts. We had a short conversation; I heard a funny story about my daddy and he let me go to my next class. What could have been really bad turned out not so bad after all.

Not bad, but not good, either, were my grandparents. They still lived south of town in the country. I still hung out a little with my grandmother in the kitchen and the garden. I also poked around granddaddy's garage workshop a little, but not much. Been there, done that.

In an effort to be the grandson I knew my granddaddy really wanted, I decided to express an interest in shooting the gun. He had already taught me how to shoot. Granddaddy took me out in the field beside the garage and gave me a few refresher lessons. He was an avid hunter, always coming in with quail or squirrels and the occasional rabbit .This time, I was not invited to go hunting with him. He would let me shoot at a target, usually a limb on a tree, but that was all. A few times I went out by myself, but I still wasn't really interested in killing anything. One time, Granddaddy let me and my girlfriend go "bird hunting." I wasn't lying when I told the principal that I had never hit anything I aimed at, so the birds were not in any danger. We just wanted to have fun. In the woods, while we were climbing a fence, the gun accidently discharged, almost hitting Susan in the foot. We were really shaken. We certainly didn't tell anyone what happened. That pretty much ended the gun phase for me, and also, Susan. There were better things for teenaged girls to do.

Years later, my granddaddy did redeem himself. I grew up, went to college, got married. By the way, Granddaddy left my wedding after the ceremony because he disapproved of its extravagance. Trust me, it was not extravagant. What he didn't know was that Mama spent years putting money aside so I could have a nice wedding. She finally saved $500 which bought my wedding gown and all the flowers. The rest was paid for out of pocket or charged.

The redeeming came a few years later. Amanda came along, his great-granddaughter. He loved that little girl to death! He always sent her a birthday card which meant that he not only knew when her birthday was, but actually went to the store and picked out a card. Wow!

Once, Amanda and I were visiting Aunt Vada and Uncle Fred in Portia. Granddaddy came down from P.B. unannounced, to see Amanda. He hugged and kissed her, bounced her on his knee, generally delighting in her presence with a big smile on his face. I hadn't seen that smile much. Aunt Vada asked him to stay for dinner, but he declined. He had to get back home. He made the approximately one hundred fifty-mile round trip to spend maybe two hours with my little girl. Later, as he lay dying, he sent my Aunt Bettye out to buy Amanda a Christmas present, a doll he had seen advertised and wanted her to have. He died three days after Christmas. When we got to P.B., the doll was there, waiting for her. I wish I had known that grandfather better.

But when I was a teenager, that grandfather was not around. And I did add to their disapproval on one occasion. One day, for some reason, Mama let me drive the car, but she was sitting right next to me. The front seat in those days was not divided by a gear shift in the middle like it is now so she was very close. We were on our way to my grandparents' house. We had to drive down highway 69 and make a rather sharp left turn onto the gravel road that went past their house. I was probably going a little too fast and also turned the corner a little too sharp.

That wouldn't have been a big deal except there was a pickup truck approaching the intersection just as I turned. I would have hit him head-on had not Mama grabbed the wheel and clamped down on the brake, crushing my foot in the process. We ended up in the ditch, not hurt, but very shaken up. We did miss the truck, but just barely. OK, maybe grazed the front bumper. The highway patrol had to be called. Mama asked the truck driver to please not mention that her fourteen-year-old daughter was driving. He was kind and kept his mouth shut. I think Mama got a ticket, or maybe just a warning. Since all this happened in sight of their house, there was no keeping it from the grandparents. In fact, I think Granddaddy came and pulled the car out of the ditch with his truck. Anyway, this little incident was just another reason for them to disapprove of not only me, but Mama.

One day, out of the blue, Mama asked me if I wanted to have a party. Is the Pope Catholic? Of course, I wanted to have a party. It would not be a birthday party, just a lets-have-fun party. She rented the Community Center, ordered food from a caterer, and borrowed a record player and records. I was allowed to invite whomever I wanted. I even got a new party dress. We danced, ate, played games, (not spin the bottle), and just generally goofed around. It was so much fun and I felt so special. I guess Mama thought I needed that.

The school year was winding down, as was Daddy's deployment in Greenland. We couldn't wait for him to be home. There hadn't been a lot of communication since sending a letter to or from the middle of the United States to Southern Greenland took a long time. Even if phone calls had been possible, they were too expensive and out of the question.

Finally, he was home, in Poplar Bluff, hugging and kissing, laughing, and talking, dispensing gifts. We were so happy to have him home. Knowing we would be living together again was the icing on the cake. Daddy got his assignment before he left Greenland. He had the usual thirty days leave before he had to report for duty in Fort Eustis, Virginia. We had been there before, living off post in Lee Hall. While we had changed, the situation at Ft. Eustis had not. As before, there were no quarters available on post. We would have to live off post in civilian housing.

The plan was that Mama and Daddy would drive to Virginia to find us a place to live while I went to Girl Scout camp. We would move when they got back and camp was over. They got time together and I got a new experience.

I had not been to resident camp before. Day camp, yes, but not ever away from home for two weeks. Camp Latonka was on Lake Wapello, just north of Poplar Bluff. It turned out to be fun. I learned to paddle a canoe, improved my swimming skills, handle a jack knife carefully, cook over a campfire, and all sorts of other camp-ish things. I also found a rare Indian ax head on the shore of the lake.

One of the challenges of resident camp was living in close quarters with other girls. There were six of us in one cabin. As an only child, I didn't have much experience with sharing my space with others. Thus, the dust-up, or, to be honest, the fight. I can't remember just what the fight was about. I think it had to do with making noise while I was trying to sleep or may have been the culmination of multiple irritations over the course of several days. Whatever it was, the initial disagreement spiraled into a knock-down, drag-out fight complete with hair pulling, biting, scratching, and kicking. The fight spilled out of the cabin into the dirt. One of the counselors broke it up. There were scratches and bruises. There were tears. And, yes, there were consequences.

The next morning both me and my opponent were called into the presence of the Camp Director. Suffice it to say, she was not happy. Brawling campers were not what she signed up for. A friend to all and a sister to every Girl Scout had gone right out the window, or in this case, the door. Since I started the fight, or at least, struck the first blow, I was in the most trouble. I was to be expelled from camp. "I will call your parents to come get you today.," she decreed. Well, no. I didn't know how to get in touch with my parents since they were in Virginia looking for a place to live. So that plan didn't fly. I got to stay but had to switch cabins, which suited me. I kept my mouth shut, but what I really wanted to say was, "But you know how to get ahold of Sassy Sally's parents. Call them." But I didn't. We apologized and promised not to come to blows again. And, yes, I was in big trouble when my parents were told of my misdeed. But we were moving on so it was basically over. No one cared.

On to Virginia—and, oh, my Lord, High School.

FORT EUSTIS, VIRGINIA

We were back at Fort Eustis in Virginia. We had been here before, back when Daddy was attending the Transportation School. Earlier, Mama and I had joined Daddy in Seattle. Then we went home to Poplar Bluff while he awaited orders to transfer to Ft. Eustis where we joined him. After graduating from the T-School, Daddy was assigned to be a Transport Commander on the Navy ships plying the Atlantic during the last years of World War II. When the war was over, we would live in New York, Arkansas, Japan, and Missouri. Now Daddy had completed his assignment in Greenland and was stationed at Ft. Eustis. Now it was 1955 and we were in Virginia again. Grade school was over for me. I was about to start high school.

What had not changed in all those years was that there were still no quarters available on post. Once again, we would live in Lee Hall. Not, this time, in the antebellum mansion turned boarding house where we lived before, but in Lee Hall, the small town that grew up around the old plantation. Our rental house was in a small subdivision at the western edge of town, across highway

60 from the old plantation fields and the small-town center.

The old Lee Hall was still there, but it was no longer a boarding house. Now it was a single-family home, belonging to the family of the lady who ran the boarding house long ago. Soon after we moved in, Mama and Daddy made a trip over there just to say hello and, I guess, catch up with the lady's family. If I knew the history of the house, I didn't appreciate it. Now I do. Early in the Civil War, during the early days of the Peninsula Campaign, it served both the Confederate and Union armies as a headquarters. That's probably the only reason it survived.

Now, it is on the National Register of Historic Places and is a tourist attraction. When my husband and I visited decades later, we arrived late in the day just as they were about to close the doors. When I mentioned that I had lived there as a little girl, the guide, who was standing in the hall with her purse on her arm, plopped it down and said, "I didn't know that this had ever been a boarding house. Ok. Let's go. We'll show each other around." And we did. She showed me things I had forgotten about the house and I showed her the room my parents rented, where my bed was and where the bathroom was down the hall and where I remembered playing on the grounds.

I only have two distinct memories of living in Lee Hall. One is of Mama and I spending the day at the beach, really on the shore of the York River on an overcast day.

She didn't know that even if the sun isn't shining, you can still get sunburned, and we did, big time. We both hurt for days. The other memory involves the couple who lived across the hall from us. He had survived the Bataan Death March in the Philippines. This particular evening, he was telling his tale and showing us his souvenirs from that time. He told us how excited all the prisoners were when the Japanese soldiers gave them eggs to eat and how they were laughed at when they discovered to their dismay that the eggs were fertilized and inedible because they had partially formed baby chicks in them. But what I remember most were his boxer shorts. He was wearing them when the march started. By the time it ended, he had patched them so much that there was no original fabric left. When I shared that memory with the guide, she just shuttered. Civil War soldiers were not the only warriors to live in Lee Hall. I think I added another dimension to her understanding of the history of the place.

But that was then, and this was now. The subdivision where we rented a house was pretty cookie-cutter. There were three streets with probably 25-30 houses. All had three bedrooms and one bathroom, an attached carport, and a clothesline in the back yard. Some had a large six-pane picture window, and some had a bank of three windows across the front of the house. We had a picture window. The panes were not fixed, they all opened out. Later, when we got an air conditioner—finally—Daddy took out the bottom center pane and installed the air conditioner. It looked ugly, but we were cool--kinda. Central air was not a thing yet.

All right, we were in Virginia, but just exactly where were we? On the Eastern Seaboard of the United States, but also in the middle of the early history of our country, that's where. We were on the Virginia Peninsula, bounded on the east by the York River and on the west by the James River. Down the peninsula, both rivers emptied into Hampton Roads, then into the final reaches of the Chesapeake Bay at Norfolk.

Ft. Eustis is on the James River, close to where our country began, in Jamestown. Across the peninsula, not too far, was Yorktown, another historic colonial settlement. Up the peninsula, again, not too far, was Colonial Williamsburg, where all sorts of things went on in the early days of our country. I didn't fully appreciate where we were at the time, but I was beginning to think it was neat to live so close to so many historic places. What more can you expect from a teenager?

In Lee Hall, almost everyone rented, and everyone was Army personnel. We might as well have been on post. When the cars pulled out of the driveways in the mornings, they all headed for the Main Gate. Even though we lived outside the gate, our lives were very much engaged with what was inside the gate. For one thing, the PX and the commissary were there, as was the Officers' Club and pool, the Chapel, and the hospital. Both Girl

Scout and Boy Scout troops met on post. The Teen Club had their meetings, (parties) there. The beauty shop served the ladies as the barber shop served the gents. Plus, many of our friends lived on post. And, of course, all the fathers worked there.

While our lives revolved around the fort, there was the town of Lee Hall that influenced our lives, too. The town was small, one main street. I remember a general store, a barber shop, post office and a church. Train tracks and Highway 60 bisected the town, putting our subdivision on the wrong side of the tracks. Also, on the wrong side of the tracks was a gas station/ convenience store which one of my onetime boyfriend's family owned, so I was there a lot. They lived above the store. He had the cutest dog. When the dog wanted to eat, he got a can of dog food off the shelf and walked around with it in his mouth until someone opened the can for him. On Sunday night, the local Baptist Church had a Teen program. Even though we went to chapel on post, most of us went to the teen program, too.

Then there was school. I would attend Warwick High school. This was the biggest school I had ever attended. There were lots of kids. It was about fifteen miles farther down the peninsula, close to Newport News and Norfolk. There was a contingent of Navy Brats as well as the Army Brats from Ft. Eustis. Yes, there was a little rivalry going on. We Army Brats were outnumbered, but we held our own. At least, I thought so.

The bus picked us up first, us being the five kids in our subdivision who attended Warwick High. We met at the Gray's house because it was close to the front, just off the highway. These were the same Grays who lived across the street from us in Yokohama. While we waited for the bus to come, we usually played Monopoly until someone turned us on to Canasta. We played a running game for weeks at a time. The Grays carport had been turned into a screened in porch, so most days we could just put the cards down and pick up the game the next morning.

Our bus driver's name was Gladys. She was not very cheerful or welcoming. I have a feeling that if she could have found something else to do rather than drive teenagers to and from school every day, she would have jumped on it. She didn't like us and we didn't like her. Behind her back, we called her Happy Ass.

The bus wound its way along the back roads on either side of the highway, picking up civilians as well as Army Brats. The contrast between the civilian and army kids was pretty big and did not make for a good mix. Neither group understood the other. There were a few fights, mostly verbal, but a few blows were struck from time to time. Happy Ass was not happy with us.

At school, we were not particularly welcome. As In Waynesville, we were held responsible for overcrowding the schools. My freshman year, I took Latin. Ugh! The teacher, whose name was also Carolyn, did not like me, so I didn't like her right back. Nor did I like her subject and subsequently was failing the class. You have heard it said,

"Latin is a dead language, as dead as it can be. First it killed the Romans, and now it's killing me."

When I got my first F, I knew I had to do something, so I went to my biology teacher to ask his advice. By the way, I had a big crush on him. He said he would speak to her on my behalf. The first class after he spoke to her, I had high hopes that maybe she would be nicer to me and I could make some strides in the right direction, like not failing the class. I was sitting in the front of the class with my book open, following along. She called on me, asking me a question, following it with, "If you even know what page we're on." I did. I even knew the answer to the question she asked. But that made me so mad, I quit. From then on, Latin class served as my study hall. I sat in the back of the room and ignored her and her class. I took the F and moved on. We never spoke again.

Freshman year was my first experience with Phys. Ed. Class. Changing clothes at school, taking a shower, all new to me. Having class outside on the playing field was different, too. One time, we were learning how to do the high jump. For the life of me, I couldn't do it. I'd get right up to the bar and stumble. After multiple failures, the gym teacher asked if I was left-handed. Yes, I was. "Then approach the bar from the left side." That worked. Apparently, if you are left -handed, you are also left-footed. Problem solved.

Since we rode the bus, we didn't get to participate in any of the after-school activities. We couldn't stay to practice with the sports teams or band or join play practice because there was no way to get home. This was the age of one-car families. Even if you were old enough to drive, you didn't have a car because Daddy drove the car to work. Now, there was a bus from the fort to the football and basketball games, but that was it. All the stuff we did after school was done on post or in Lee Hall.

Of course, there was a Girl Scout troop for me to join. Since I was now in high school, the troop would ordinarily have been a Senior troop, but this was a Mariner troop, befitting our residence on the Eastern Seaboard where naval activities were all around us. Our uniforms were not the usual green, but a blue blouse with the square navy collar and a blue skirt. Unlike grade school, I did not wear my uniform to school. It was not cool.

What was cool was our troop leader. Like at Ft. Wood, she was not one of our moms, the usual leader, but a young Army wife who grew up as a Girl Scout, so she knew the ropes. Her husband's last post had been Ft.

Belvoir, near Washington, D.C. It so happened that they went to the same chapel where the Eisenhower clan attended. In fact, she had been Sunday School teacher to some of the Eisenhower grandkids. The two families had formed a bond, which turned out to be really good for our troop.

Even though wearing my uniform to school was not cool, I did wear it proudly when the troop went on outings. And there were several of them. The first I remember was a trip to Jamestown to see the newly-arrived replicas of the three ships that brought the first settlers to Jamestown—the Susan Constant, Godspeed, and the Discovery. They were exact replicas except for their size. They were a little smaller than the originals. The arrival of these ships was a big deal for the Virginia Peninsula. The ships were unique. They expanded the understanding of Jamestown and created the desire of tourists to visit. We were excited to see them.

We arrived in Jamestown on a Saturday morning, dressed in our Mariner uniforms. We were invited aboard the Susan Constant and given a VIP tour, even got to take a swing on the rigging, just like real sailors. We also got our pictures taken and appeared in the Sunday addition of the Newport News newspaper. Big deal, at least to us.

Another outing I remember fondly was a father-daughter fishing trip, no uniforms this time. Our leader's husband was in charge. It must have been his idea. I don't remember exactly where we went, somewhere on the York River, probably some fishing pier. I do remember Daddy teaching me how to bait a hook, and, when I caught a fish, how to unhook the fish without hooking my finger. It was one of those special days that sticks in your head. For Army Brats, our fathers were not always a constant in our lives because they were sometimes stationed where we couldn't be together, so time together was important.

Like all Girl Scouts, we worked on badges. When you got to be a Senior Scout, the goal was to earn the Curved Bar rank. This is the same thing as the Boy Scouts Eagle Scout rank. Earning the honor was hard. It took a lot of work and a lot of time. The last badge I had to earn was the Conservation Badge. One of the requirements was that I had to maintain a bird feeder and keep track of and identify the birds who came to the feeder. Daddy built me a bird feeder and we put it in the back yard just outside the kitchen window. Propped on the windowsill above the kitchen sink was a Birds of North America book so we could look up which birds were frequenting the feeder. I had to use part of my allowance to buy bird food and keep the feeder full. This turned out to be a family project. All three of us learned to identify the birds. In fact, from then on, the Hornbuckles fed the birds, and a few squirrels, wherever we lived.

Several members of the troop earned the Curved Bar rank. Since it was a big deal, we had a special Awards Ceremony. Our parents were invited as well as members of the Council Staff and Board. Our fathers pinned the award on our uniforms. Then, our leader informed us that she had received a special letter addressed to all the recipients of the Curved Bar. It was from Mrs. Eisenhower! She mentioned each of us by name and offered congratulations from herself and the President. We were blown away! What troop of Girl Scouts gets a letter from the First Lady? We did!

But we weren't through with the Eisenhowers. After school was out for the summer, we were going on a road trip to Gettysburg. Our leader and her husband were both graduates of Gettysburg College so going there was a no-brainer. We would visit the battlefield and the campus. Visiting the campus meant visiting not only the classrooms and dorms, but also the sorority and fraternity houses. We girls were particularly interested in the frat houses. Also, on the agenda was a trip out to the Eisenhower's farm. There was a chance they would be there since the farm was their sanctuary from the political life in Washington, D.C.

There was a gate complete with MPs at the farm. We were told that the limo was on the way, in fact, it would be there soon. So, we lined up on either side of the drive, smart in our Mariner uniforms, and waited. Pretty soon, here it came, the Presidential limo. Was it Ike or Mamie? Or both? As the limo approached, we stood at attention and saluted. Mamie was in the car which paused long enough for her to wave at us, then went on through the gate. Even though the encounter was brief, we were thrilled. That was the highlight of our visit, even beating out our interaction—read flirting—with the frat boys at the Kappa Sig house.

There was one other place where we got to wear our uniforms and stand out from the crowd. During the school year, we volunteered at the Mariner's Museum in Newport News. We welcomed visitors, handed out brochures, and mostly pointed out where the restrooms were. As an aside, we got to tell people about Mariner Scouts because there was a lot of curiosity about these teenage girls in blue. I was sorry when we moved and I had to join a regular Senior Troop.

As is usual, our troop sold Girl Scout cookies. In those days, we sold door-to-door. The cookies were ordered ahead of time and when they came, we took what we thought we could sell and hit the streets, knocking on doors, and plying what we had been taught about salesmanship. Don't say, "Do you want to buy some Girl Scout cookies?" because the easy answer was "No." Instead, you said, "I have Girl Scout cookies. How many boxes do you want?" It worked. We also had to learn how to make change, which was hard for me. Whatever cookies were left over, we sold at a booth, usually outside the PX or Commissary.

This first cookie sale at Ft. Eustis was different. I had all my cookies and was ready to go, but I got sick. So sick that I had to be hospitalized. What to do? We only had so much time to sell our cookies. Well, Daddy stepped in to save the day. He took the cookies to work with him. His office was in a barracks which was, of course, full of hungry soldiers. He ended up being the troop's highest seller!

There's a little more to the story. I don't really remember what my diagnosis was, but I had a very high fever. To get it down, the doctor ordered me to drink a gallon of grapefruit juice in an hour. I hated grapefruit, and its juice. Could I switch to something else? No, it had to be grapefruit juice. Mama helped me get the job done. I gagged and cried the whole hour. And while I hated that doctor, it worked. My fever went down and the next day I got to go home. Never do I want to do that again. To this day, I hate grapefruit. I'd have much rather been selling cookies.

But I wasn't the only one who landed in the hospital while we were at Ft. Eustis. Daddy had contracted malaria when he was working for his father in the summer between his freshman and sophomore years at the University of Missouri. The project was draining the sunk lands in Northeast Arkansas. The sunk lands were the result of the New Madrid earthquake in 1811. Reelfoot Lake was not the only land that sank. All over the area around New Madrid there were lakes and swamps. My granddad was basically draining the swamps and digging drainage ditches to hold the water and move it away from land that could grow crops, in this case, cotton. Those ditches are still there.

You don't have swamps without mosquitoes, and if there are mosquitoes, there is most likely malaria. Daddy got malaria that summer and it stayed with him the rest of his life, periodically raising its ugly head, and putting him in the hospital. This time he was really sick, so was hospitalized for several days. I would take the Ft. Eustis bus from school so I could see Daddy. Mama was there, of course, keeping him company. We stayed with him and helped him with his dinner, then went home. We were not allowed to stay, anyway. I think he had at least one more bout with malaria in his lifetime. It just never truly went away.

Now, our proximity to Williamsburg meant that we were there often, not just as tourists, but as locals who came to shop and to eat. Near the end of Duke of Gloucester Street was a neat ice cream shop where we always stopped when we were in town. Williamsburg is also a college town so that meant that there was a demand for formal wear, prom dresses, bridal gowns, etc. I was going to my first prom, so Mama and I went to Williamsburg to shop. After looking at several dresses, I found one that I absolutely adored. It was so pretty! Mama looked at the price tag and said that it was too expensive. We would have to go down to Newport News to see if we could find one that wasn't so costly. I was really disappointed. I loved that dress, but it was what it was and I just had to accept it.

Several days later, when Daddy and I got home from work and Scouts, I walked into my bedroom and, there, laying out on my bed, was The Dress! I screamed. Daddy had not been clued in and thought something awful had happened. He charged into my bedroom to rescue me, only to find me clutching the dress like a long-lost child. I was so happy. He was a little bit miffed. Mama stepped in and calmed the situation. I don't know what

Mama did to afford that dress, but I was so grateful. I wore it many times, certainly got the value out of it. It hangs in my closet to this day.

Soon after we got to Lee Hall, we decided that we would go to dinner at the King's Arms Tavern in Williamsburg. It served meals just like in colonial days. We thought it would be neat to experience a little of the colonial vibe. Our meal was excellent, the service suburb. As we were finishing dessert, the waiter sat bowls of a clear liquid in front of us. What was this? Wasn't dessert the end of dinner? No one around us had these bowls. We stared at them in confusion. Just as Daddy was hesitantly picking up his spoon, Mama gasped, "It's a finger bowl!" She saved us! We cleaned our fingers just like we knew what we were doing and beat a hasty exit. Now, it's funny. Then, not so much.

Our dining adventures did not stop at the King's Arms. I had started babysitting in the neighborhood. Often, the couple would go out for pizza. What was pizza? Some Italian dish. It boggles the mind to think that there was a time when people in the United States didn't know what pizza was. But we didn't and decided to find out. Just across from the Main Gate was a restaurant the served pizza. So, one evening after work, Mama, Daddy, and I went to try it out. The waitress brought us a menu which we perused with not much understanding. Since it was early, we were almost the only customers in the place. No one else had been served. Daddy told the waitress, "We're going to have pizza. Three pizzas, please" She looked at us, assessed the situation and kindly suggested that she bring us only one. They were big, but if we wanted more, we could order more. Only when the pizza came did we understand what eating pizza entailed. And we did like it. We were hooked, just like everyone else.

On post, there was the Teen Club. I didn't go often, no transportation. But my Lee Hall friends and I did make it to some of the dances and always went on post to catch the bus to the Warwick High football games.

This was the fifties. We didn't go to school with black kids. Although I had actually gone to school with black kids in Yokohama, that was an exception, certainly not the rule. I don't even know where the black kids at Ft. Eustis went to school. There was beginning to be talk about desegregation. The Supreme Court ruling was in 1954, but nobody was exactly jumping on that bandwagon, at least, not in Virginia. My friends and I agreed that segregation was wrong, and something ought to be done about it. Only those of us who had gone to school overseas had ever gone to school with black kids. We knew those kids were no different than us. Our education had not been compromised in any way, form, or fashion by having black kids in our classrooms. My friends and I felt good about how we felt. Hey, we were kind, caring, liberal, and, yes, kinda smug. But one night it all came crashing down on me.

We were at a dance at the Teen Club. My girlfriends and I were standing on the sidelines, probably trying to observe how one actually danced to rock and roll. There was a group of black boys also on the sidelines. They were laughing among themselves, with a few side glances at us. Then one of them left the group and approached me.

He held out his hand and said, "Do you want to dance with me?"

I instantly froze in shock. What? "NO," I said, and turned away.

He just shrugged and went back to his friends. They laughed at him. I think he probably asked me on a bet and lost. No big surprise that the white girl turned him down.

But this white girl was devasted at what she had done. Push came to shove, and I failed, big time. All my high-faultin' talk about equality and fairness, etc., etc., went right out the window. I said no to the opportunity to make a statement. Actually, my no was a statement, the usual one in our culture. Whites and blacks do not interact, certainly not on a dance floor. I was embarrassed at myself. Oh, how I wish, even to this day, that I could take back that no and apologize to that black boy. I wonder how, if at all, he remembers that encounter.

There were other places to go on post where the results were more positive. One place was the pool at the Officers' Club. In the summer, my friend Charlotte Savage and I went almost every day. Either Daddy or her mother gave us a ride. Sometimes our boyfriends, friends who were boys, not romantic interests, joined us.

` Classes were offered in Lifesaving by the lifeguards, handsome young lieutenants who were way out of our wheelhouse, but we could dream, and did. There was also an exercise class that involved swimming laps and a little water aerobics, and then there was sunbathing. That was the best part. We sat around in the sun and did nothing. Our goal was to get as tan as possible. This was before we started getting information that exposure to the sun was bad for you, caused cancer and other bad things. I don't think sunscreen even existed. To get tan, we put on a mixture of iodine and baby oil. Put some iodine in a bottle of baby oil, shake it up and spread it on. That was the magic elixir to make us deeply tan. And it worked! We were seriously tan.

There was one thing that bothered me about the pool. If the timing was right, at the end of the day, and we were in the car leaving the pool, when taps were played, the car had to stop and we had to get out, face the flag, and salute. That was fine. What was not fine was that we had on our bathing suits and always got whistled at and stared at by the soldiers who were in the area and saw us. I was always embarrassed because Daddy heard them.

The Officers" Club offered other amenities other than the pool. We could go to dinner there, mostly after Chapel on Sunday. Mama and her friends gathered there to play bridge. My Girl Scout troop was once invited to high tea by the Officers' Wives Club. It was special.

One time, in the summer, the West Point cadets came to the fort. As part of their education, the cadets toured various military installations to see how the real Army worked. When they were on post, there was always a formal dance. The daughters of the officers were invited. There were strict rules. The daughter had to be escorted to the dance by her father, in uniform. Daddy and I were greeted at the door by the officer in charge, who assured Daddy that his daughter would be well taken care of and he could pick her up promptly at ten o'clock. All the girls were paired with a cadet who was approximately her height. That was the standard, not too tall, not too short. Hopefully, the height match would lead to a social match as well. My cadet and I hit it off. We were both a little shy but managed to enjoy the evening. I was asked to dance by some of the other cadets, too. All in all, it was a nice evening. I'm glad I got to experience it.

Another experience I'm glad I had was our trip down to Norfolk on a Sunday afternoon. The USS Forrestal had just been christened the day before and the public was invited to come aboard and look around. It was a chilly December day, but I didn't mind. There are not too many opportunities to walk around on an aircraft carrier, at least, not then. I remember walking on the dock up to the ship, thinking how big it was. Then, as we walked up the gangplank, it just got bigger and bigger. The flight deck just went on and on. It was just overwhelming. I'm so glad Daddy insisted that we go.

But I was not through with the Navy and its ships. Summer between freshman and sophomore years, I went with the Grays when they stayed a week at Ft. Story. Ft. Story is the Army's share of Virginia Beach. Higher ranking officers like Col. Gray could rent a beach house on post. Jan and I enjoyed the beach, swimming in the surf, and playing ball with the little Grays, but we were teenagers, so we went exploring on our own, no siblings, no parents. At Virginia Beach there is an amusement park, so we rode the rides, played a few games, and shopped a little. Then we happened upon an auction. Neither of us had ever been to an auction, so we took a seat to see what went on. Jan bid on something but didn't win, thank heavens, because he didn't have the money to pay for it. But it was fun.

One day that week, something happened that was, to say the least, unusual. The entire Atlantic fleet steamed out of the Port of Norfolk. I don't know why, what was up, if anything, but all day, from dawn to dusk, ships large and small sailed out of Hampton Roads, right by where we were staying. I have no idea where they went. We didn't see them come back to port. All in all, it was quite a sight to see.

It wasn't often that we reconnected with people we knew, but I somehow reconnected with my best friend from Ft. Wood, Henegg Henderson. Her daddy was now stationed at Fort Belvoir. It was arranged that she should come for a visit. We were both so happy to see each other. She stayed for a week. I introduced her to my friends, we went to the pool, and just hung out. One day, she decreed that it was time for me to pluck my eyebrows. They needed shaping, and she would see to it. She got some tweezers from my mama, who didn't object. She laid me out on the bed and went to work. My word! I thought she would kill me! It hurt so much. But when it was over, and I had survived, I did have nicely shaped big girl eyebrows.

We put Henegg on a bus to D.C. with the promise that I would visit soon. And, in a few weeks, I was on a bus and headed north. The first thing I remember seeing was the Iwo Jima Memorial in a round-about at Ft. Belvoir's front gate. But there was a lot more to come. All week, we toured Washington, D.C. I saw all the sights--- the Washington Monument, Lincoln Memorial, Capitol, White House, the Smithsonian, and the changing of the guard at the Tomb of the Unknown Soldier. The only place where we actually went inside was the Smithsonian. There was so much to take in. I do remember the Kitty Hawk and some Neanderthal Man exhibit.

Then it was off to the amusement park where we rode the roller coaster and all the other terrifying rides.

Altogether, it was a wonderful visit. I hated to go home. We parted in tears. Soon after, her daddy was transferred, and not long after that, my daddy was transferred, too. We lost touch. But I treasure my memories and my friendship with Henegg.

But there were experiences I was not glad I had. One Saturday night I was at Jan's house. The Grays were at my house playing bridge with my parents. Jan and I were babysitting his younger brother and sister. I don't know what we were doing. The Gray's didn't have a TV yet. Probably just sitting around talking. Anyway, suddenly we heard a loud crash coming from the highway in front of the house. Jan looked out the door to see a car wrapped around a telephone pole just down the street. We both grabbed our jackets—it was cold—and ran to the scene. We were the first people there.

It was bad. The driver was slumped over the steering wheel, dead. The front seat passenger was hanging out of the car, badly injured. The guy in the back seat was not so seriously hurt. We helped him out of the car. He walked around, with his head in his hands, stumbling and moaning. Then we pulled the front seat passenger out of the car and laid him on the ground. He was not breathing so we started CPR. In Scouts, we were taught that the first thing you do is make sure the airway is clear is to tilt the head back. The way you did this was by putting your hand in the mouth, grabbing the front teeth, and pulling up. When I did this, his front teeth came out in my hand! I was so shocked I could hardly move, so Jan started compressions. When I got my wits about me, I took over so Jan could tend to the other guy. By that time, other people had showed up.

There was one lady who kept trying to get me to stop CPR. In fact, several of the adults were taking exception to a couple of teenagers commanding the scene. But we knew what we were doing, ignored them, and kept on doing it. At some point, both Jan and I put our jackets under the guy we were working on because it was so cold. He did start breathing, but it was labored. Finally, the Highway Patrol showed up followed by an ambulance. All three guys were taken away and a tow truck showed up to move the car. It was technically over, except it wasn't. We were really shaken up. Jan walked me home, his arm around my shoulders. The minute we stepped into the house, I started wailing. Jan told our parents what had happened. Mama put me to bed and the Grays went home.

The next morning the news told us that the guy we tried to save died on the way to the hospital. All three were soldiers, stationed at Ft. Eustis. They were just out for a good time on a Saturday night. They were barely older than we were. All were drunk.

One of the outcomes of the incident, or so we thought, was that we both lost our Warwick High School jackets since they went with the guy in the ambulance.

Almost everyone at school had a Warwick High jacket. They were the school colors-magenta and gold, with our first names embroidered on the front above the pocket. A week later, after school, there was a knock on our door. It was the Highway Patrolman who had worked the accident. He returned my jacket and Jan's. He had taken the trouble to contact the school to see who Carrie and Jan were and where we lived. He even had the jackets cleaned. That was, by far, the best thing about the whole incident.

When I turned sixteen, now in Paducah, I did not high tail it down to the DMV to get my driver's license. The whole thing haunted me still, especially the guy's teeth coming out in my hand. Finally, when I was seventeen, I got my driver's license. Even after all these years, I have not forgotten that terrible night.

But life moves on, and so did I. My friends and I did date even though no one in my crowd was old enough to drive. When we went out, we were chauffeured by one of our fathers. Mostly, we went to the movies on post or to the Teen Club. One-time Jan and I and Charlotte and her date went to Norfolk to see Elvis Presley's first movie, Love Me Tender. By the way, most of our parents were not big fans of Elvis. Nevertheless, Col. Gray drove us down to the show. I'm pretty sure he did not go to the movie. But he picked us up when it was over. When we were on a date in the car, the couple always sat in the back seat. That way, we could sneak in a few kisses if we were quiet.

We really believed that the dad driver didn't know what was going on. Silly us!

Then there was the problem of saying good night at the end of the date. Dad was in the car, watching. The girl and boy gave each other a "I'd love to kiss you but dad is watching." look, squeezed hands and that was it. The older kids with a driver's license and access to a car, usually ended their dates over at a park on the York River where they "watched the submarine races," our code for necking. I never got to do that. Darn!

We had nice neighbors, most of whom we knew. We certainly greeted one another coming and going. Directly across the street lived three Chaplains, all Catholic. We really didn't see them often. They weren't exactly in our circle. Once I saw one of them do a part of his calling I'm sure he didn't relish. He was with a couple of MPs in a staff car. They knocked on the door of a house at the end of the street. When that happens, you know something bad has happened. And it had. There had been an accident involving a tank and a truck and the man of the house was dead. When the crying and screaming were over, I watched the Chaplin walk home, his head down and his shoulders slumped. Not a good day in the neighborhood. All the neighbors stepped up, Mama included, and did what they could to help.

I had friends on the street. Hunter Swisher lived two doors down. Oh, he was so handsome! He was a grade ahead of me. We never dated, were just good friends. Across the street from Hunter lived my friend Charlotte Savage. She didn't have a father, for which I was always sorry. He had died unexpectedly of a heart attack two years before. It was just she and her mom and a younger brother. Her older sister lived close. Her dad died on the eve of her sister's wedding. They went ahead with it, as he would have wanted. The sister walked down the aisle by herself. Her brother met her at the alter to give her away. They buried him in his tuxedo. Instead of renting one, he just bought one because, he said, he still had two more weddings to go so he thought he would get his money's worth. How sad.

Our neighbors on one side included a boy my age and his little brother. Dad was a stern father. He ran a tight ship. I had seen his kind before, in Yokohama and in Ft. Wood. Nevertheless, the ship leaked a little because Wayne, that was his name, was likely to slip out of the bedroom window in the middle of the night. I don't think he ever did anything bad. He just roamed around the neighborhood. His little brother always helped him crawl back in the window, quietly. But somehow his dad found out and the result was that Wayne was sent to Military School. I think it was Fork Union, which wasn't too far away.

Several times when the family would go to visit him, they would invite me to come along. Wayne and I were always given some time alone so we could talk. I would catch him up on our friends at home and on what was happening at school. In retrospect, I think I may have been being promoted as a future daughter-in-law. Not me. While I liked Wayne, I wanted no part of his family.

Our other next-door neighbors, the Spinozas, were a young family with two little boys. I babysat for them a lot. Carla was from Biloxi. I think Juan, we called him John, grew up in Cuba. They introduced us to something she grew up doing—going crabbing. Not only the Gulf Coast, but the Eastern Seaboard has its share of crabs and we were going to learn how to catch them.

We went over to the York River, to where a small stream emptied into the York. It was shallow and wide, with a sand bar in the middle, very wadable. There are two ways you can catch a crab. You can just scoop him up in a long-handled net, if you're fast enough, or you can lure him in to your net by tying a meaty bone on a string, throwing it out in the stream, and, when the crab comes up to have a bite, you slowly pull the bone, so he will follow it, until you get him under your long-handled net. Then you yank it up and he's caught! It takes a little practice to master the procedure, but very much worth it.

Each family had a big peach basket to hold our crabs. When it was full enough, we'd quit for the day and head home. Mama boiled them up and all three of us would sit around the kitchen table picking out crab meat.

It was a slow process, really a pain, but we knew what was coming, delicious crab cakes, which were worth the effort.

One day, there was an unexpected bonus to the crabbing. Daddy forgot and left the bait, those meaty bones, in the trunk of the car. Naturally, with the summer heat, it didn't take long for the smell to get really bad. When Daddy opened the trunk, he reeled back from the smell. Mama began teasing him about the smell and about forgetting to discard the bones. After he threw away the bones, he got out the hose to wash out the trunk, not the best idea. The teasing escalated, and the next thing I knew, Daddy was chasing Mama around the front yard, spraying her with the hose. In retaliation, she got out another hose and started spraying him. They were running all over the place, laughing and just having a good time.

This scene has always stayed with me and I treasure it. I knew my parents loved each other, but there it was, love running around the yard, getting wet, not caring, enjoying each other, sharing the moment.

Something else I got from the Spinozas was a summer romance. Carla's younger brother, Denny, came to spend the summer with them. He was two years older, a nice Southern boy. I was smitten from the start. We spent as much time together as we could. He was mowing lawns and I was babysitting when Charlotte and I weren't at the pool. We did manage to go out, as well as make out, a little. Maybe more than a little. It was a nice summer romance, more than nice. But, like all summer romances, it came to an end. When he got on that bus back to Biloxi, my heart just broke. We wrote a few letters back and forth, but that soon dwindled to nothing and it was over. I still have the memories, though.

When I was a sophomore, we finally got a television set! TV had been around since I was at least in first grade, but it was not available everywhere because the TV stations didn't have much broadcasting power. In Brooklyn, there was TV, because I remember watching Howdy Dowdy at the neighbor's house. There was no TV in Portia or Yokohama, but there was TV in PB, but we couldn't afford one. No TV in Ft. Wood because it was in the middle of nowhere. Still couldn't afford one when Mama and I went back to PB. But there was TV in Lee Hall. There were at least three TV stations we could watch—one in Norfolk, one in Richmond, and one in D.C. It was black and white, and went off the air at night, and you had to get up and walk to the TV to change the channel, but it was TV.

Daddy and I liked to watch Jimmy Dean, yes, the sausage king, in the morning as we got dressed for the day. He had a country variety show on the D.C. channel. Daddy and I went back and forth between the bedrooms and the bathroom to the TV room which was the third bedroom in the house, decorated to be a child's nursery.

The landlord wouldn't let us paint it, so we lived with it. The TV was not in the living room where you'd think it would be because Mama didn't want that "thing" in the living room, so, it wasn't.

For a while, Daddy and I shared something we would rather not have—boils. If you've ever had one you know how awful they are. They hurt, they're ugly, they ooze with pus, and no one wants to be around you, lest you transmit the nasty thing to them. Daddy got one on his face, then the next week I got one on my leg. We were both shaving those parts of our bodies, but not sharing a razor, so I don't know how the boils got from one to the other. We were careful, but before it was over, we each had four boils. Ugh! Yuk!

Despite the difficulties, our two years at Ft. Eustis were good years. I became a full-fledged teenager. I had my hair cut in a duck tail, all the rage, wore white bucks and/or saddle shoes, lace collars with my sweaters and a gold necklace. I took up smoking. Mama smoked cigarettes; Daddy smoked a pipe. This was before we knew anything about smoking being bad for you. By the way, I'm paying for it now. I was a good student, except for Latin, a baby-sitter, and a Curved Bar Rank Girl Scout. I got along with my parents and didn't swear, at least not much, and never in front of them. What more could you want from a fifteen-year-old?

Daddy was transferred to recruiting duty in Paducah, Kentucky. He was still a Captain, so he was over age in grade, which meant that he was too old to still be a captain. The reason he had not been promoted was, basically, because he didn't always get a good review on his performance report. He didn't always keep his mouth shut. When he should have said, "Yes, Sir," and smiled, he instead expressed his conflicting opinion. Not the thing that got you a good report, so, no promotion.

He would finish out his twenty years as a Master Sergeant on recruiting duty. I think he only had four more years to go as he retired when I was in college. When he retired, he was promoted to Major with a Major's pay grade.

We were moving again. Again, Mama and Daddy were going ahead of me. I was going to Girl Scout camp near Roanoke, Virginia to be a Counselor-in-Training. I would be there a month. They went to Paducah and bought a house. That was different. We always lived in Army housing or rented. When my time at camp was over, I rode a Greyhound bus to Paducah. Another place, another school, another church, new friends. Same-o-same-o.

PADUCAH—THE LAST STOP

I arrived in Paducah on a Greyhound bus. Daddy met me at the depot and drove me to our new house. I was excited to finally be there after a month at Girl Scout camp. They were moved in and settled. My bedroom was set up and waiting for me.

The house wasn't special, but it was just what we needed. It had two bedrooms and one bathroom, a living room, dining room, kitchen, and a kitchen nook that had several different uses over the years. Now it housed the washing machine. There was an attic that we accessed by pulling down the disappearing stairs in the kitchen ceiling. There wasn't a garage, but the car could be parked in back because there was an alley down the middle of the block. Later, there was a garage, where, I remember Mama stored extra supplies and clothes when there was a report that the New Madrid fault was likely to come to life and cause a big earthquake.

The neighborhood was very middle class. 2714 Monroe Street was one block removed from Jefferson Avenue, the main drag from downtown. One block up, on Joe Clifton Drive, was a big racetrack for harness racing, so we always heard horses neighing and crowds roaring

194

when it was race season. There were also lots of flies, because, horse stables equal flies. Where Joe Clifton and Jefferson Ave. met, there was a big statue of Alben Barkley, who had been Vice President of the United States under Harry Truman. He was pretty much Paducah's claim to fame, except for the fact that at the beginning of the Civil War, Paducah had surrendered to Gen. Grant without a shot being fired. That was claim to fame or claim to shame, depending on which side you were on.

As I got older, I was beginning to appreciate history and what it meant to where you were. Paducah is an old town with lots of history. Even before it was a town, it was a stopping place for people moving west. That's because it sits on the Ohio River and is where the Tennessee River empties into the Ohio River. Up river, not too far, the Cumberland River also empties into the Ohio. With that many rivers, there was a lot of stuff coming and going to and from Paducah. It was a busy river port.

The town literally bumped up to the Ohio River. At the end of the main street, and some of the other streets, all you had to do was drive through the flood wall and there was the river. The flood wall is the protector of Paducah. When the river gets high, the flood gates go up to seal off the town from the river. This was not always so. There were lots of floods, but the one in 1938 was the last straw. It was so bad that the waters were said to have reached Joe Clifton Drive. That's twenty-seven blocks from the river. Our house would have been at the edge of the river! As a result, the Corps of Engineers erected the flood wall. Now, it not only protects the town, but serves as a canvas for spectacular murals that tell the history of Paducah.

Daddy was now a Recruiting Sergeant. His office was on the second floor of the Post Office building downtown. No one else was assigned recruiting duty. It was just him. His area was all of Western Kentucky. He drove a khaki-colored staff car. He called on all the high schools and colleges and got to know all the Principals and Counselors who worked with him to identify kids who might profit from a tour of Army duty. Some kids joined because they were patriots who wanted to serve their country, many times emulating their fathers. Some kids wanted to go to college and couldn't afford it, so they joined to take advantage of the GI Bill. Some just wanted to get out of Dodge. Their home life was not good, and they needed a change. And, yes, there were a few who were given the choice, go to jail or go to the Army. There were a few who were afraid they would be drafted and end up as cannon fodder in the infantry. If you choose to join, then you had choices of what your Army tour would entail.

Years later, at Daddy's funeral, one young man told my mama, "Sarge saved my life. I was headed down a rabbit hole and he pulled me back, got me to join the

Army, and that changed my life." Mama was so grateful to hear that. When Daddy got the recruiting assignment, we did not really appreciate the dimensions of the job.

When a young man wanted to join the Army, he had to come to Daddy's office to sign up. Part of the process was giving the young man a test. Among other things, it involved recognizing various tools and what they were used for. Early on, Daddy was frustrated because so many of the guys failed the test. How could a red-blooded American boy not know what snip-nosed pliers were and how to use them? He brought the test home and had me take it. I passed with flying colors. Probably the result of all the hours I spent playing in my Granddaddy Hornbuckle's workshop. He finally took a Sears-Roebuck tool catalogue to work so he could educate the prospective recruits about tools and their uses.

I would attend Paducah Tilghman High School. It was not as large as Warwick High, but was within walking distance of the house, which was a plus. There were not too many plusses at Tilghman. All the little social groups were closed. They had been together for years, probably since grade school, and did not want newcomers encroaching on their comfort zone. The boys were better than the girls, but most of them followed the girls' lead.

There were a few nice girls. We always had lunch together, and I was welcome. But I wanted to hang out with the society girls, you know, the popular ones, the ones with money, the ones everyone knew and wanted to be. Well, they certainly wanted no part of me. For one thing, I lived in the wrong part of town. All the up-scale neighborhoods were on the other side of Joe Clifton Drive, farther out. My father was not a high-powered businessman, but a mere Army recruiter who was trying to get their brothers or boyfriends to join the Army. And I certainly did not know anyone who mattered in the town's social circles. So, no Carolyn.

These girls were mean. When it was time, later in the year, for the Junior Class to work on putting on the Junior-Senior Prom, I volunteered, hoping for some acceptance. Wrong move. They wouldn't listen to any of my ideas about decorating the cafeteria. Nor did they really ask me to take part in what they were doing. I could see them talking about me, glancing my way, and laughing. That pretty much clinched it for me. If Paducah Tilghman, Class of 1959, had a reunion across the street, I would not attend.

But I did ultimately make some friends. Of course, I joined a Girl scout troop. Our leader was one of the girl's mothers. She pretty much let us do what we wanted. It was more than nice to be part of a group, who, every time we met, raised our hands, and promised to be a friend to all and a sister of every Girl Scout. We did work on badges some. We did go camping some weekends, learned new songs, had sleepovers, started learning to cook. It was a nice, comfortable group. When Junior year was over, I went back to Virginia for another stay at camp to be a CIT, so when I was old enough to get a job, I was ready. At the end of Senior year, the whole troop would go to the Girl Scout Round-up in Colorado which was really a special experience.

Some classes at Tilghman were alright, some less so. My history class was more than OK. I was beginning to love history, particularly after my history teacher pointed out that history is a story of people's lives. She was great. She didn't insist that we learn exact dates. She thought it was more important that we be able to place events in relation to one another. She made history come alive and I really liked that.

I thought English class was going to be OK, too. It was, until the end of the first six weeks. The day of the six weeks test, I was not feeling well. Mama kept me home from school, so I missed the test.

Miss Bartlett was a good teacher. She really knew her subject and made it interesting. She was hard, demanded our attention. When I went back to school the next day, I asked her if I could take the test during class so I wouldn't have to stay after school. She said no, so I came in after school and took the test.

In the coming days, I noticed that she wasn't calling on me. Even though I raised my hand, sometimes the only one with my hand raised, she ignored me. Would this effect my grade? I so wanted to get an A. So, I went to the teacher who ran the food stand at the football games. I had signed up to work and she took me on, assigning me to count the soft drink cups and keep the stand stocked. Not much of a job, but at least I had something to do. There were a lot of kids working the stand that she had to keep busy.

When I told her that Miss Bartlett had not called on me since I asked to take the test during class, she recommended that I apologize to her. Apologize for what, I did not know, but I went in early the next morning and approached her when no one else was around. I said that I was sorry if I had offended her in any way, that was not my intention when I asked to take the test during class. She did not accept my apology. She was actually pretty dismissive of the whole thing, really rude. And, no, she still did not call on me in class. If I knew the answer to her question, I would raise my hand, to no effect. There was this one kid, a football player, who sat slumped down at the back of the class, praying that she would not call on him while I was praying that she would call on me to answer the question or go to the blackboard to finish diagramming the sentence. No such luck.

On the very last day of school, she had been teaching us how to address a letter, she asked "What is the last thing you do before posting a letter?" She had told us to wait to put the stamp on until you were sure you had everything right so if something was not right, you wouldn't waste a stamp if something had to be changed. I raised my hand, and she called on me! I was so astounded that I could hardly get the answer out. I guess that was her way of saying good-by and good riddance. I echoed the thought.

I had to take Chemistry. If I had had a choice, I would have chosen something else, but I had to have so many science credits to apply for college. The class was OK. I got the lecture part, how things are made, what was involved in putting elements together. I could even do the lab work. But for the life of me, I could not balance an equation, essential math for chemistry. The math just went right over my head. This was as bad as algebra, which also went right over my head. By this time, Senior year, I was dating Jack, who could balance an equation. He would try to help me, but with little success. One time we were at his house doing homework, when his daddy came home from work. Papa Green sat down with me and made sense of the whole thing. I was able to balance that equation, at least long enough to take the test.

What I could do was write our assignments on how a chemistry process worked. The rule was, as you are writing the process, you could not write, "and then." It had to be something else, like, "the next step is." Or "Proceed to add." Jack could not write anything to save his life. So, I helped him and he helped me and we both passed Chemistry.

I decided to try out for a play. That was not something I could do at Warwick High because of the lack of transportation, but since I could walk home, that wasn't an issue. So, I read for a part, and didn't get it. But I did get to be part of the stage crew, working on props. Even though I wasn't on stage, I knew that theatre was something I wanted to do. I was hooked, and remain hooked to this day. It is so much fun.

Something I had not expected when I moved to Paducah was that I would meet my future husband, but I did. And, honestly, I don't remember, even though I should, the first time we met, nor our first kiss, which was most likely on the front porch after a date. I think we first met at church and not at school.

My parents had already chosen a church by the time I got there. They chose Baptist Tabernacle Church. This was not the big Baptist church downtown. This was an offshoot of that church. Years ago, there had been a controversy involving playing cards. We never knew if it was poker or bridge or just cards in general. Anyway, those who did not think a friendly game of bridge was a sin broke off from First Church and started their own. Thus, Baptist Tabernacle.

It was a nice church. We were very welcome. The Greens were members there. Didn't take long for Daddy to start teaching Sunday School. He taught an Intermediate class of boys in Junior High and Freshman and Sophomore in high school. The classes moved up to the next level in December. So, Jack was in Daddy's class. When we joined, I was put in the Jr.-Sr. high school class, so when he moved up, I was already there.

We were now in the same group, but never really went to Sunday School together, because, in those days, boys and girls did not attend class together. We had a brief opening gathering, and then split up in separate classes. We did go to a Sunday School Valentine's Day dinner and sat together. I think that's the first time we really got to know each other.

Jack always told this story. He said that one Sunday he was sitting in the car outside of church and he saw me cross the street. He said to himself, "I'm going to marry that girl someday." I never believed him but he swore it was the truth.

Here's another story. Our parents got to know each other and it wasn't too long before they were regularly playing bridge together. Jack and I spoke at church but there really was no connection. I was dating other guys. Jack was dating his ham radio. I really think, no, I know, that at some point our parents decided that we should have a date. They always denied it. It was totally Jack's idea. Yeah, right.

When the call came, I wasn't at home. I had been sent to the grocery store to get a loaf of bread. Daddy answered the phone. Did Jack say, "This is Jack Green.

May I speak to Carolyn?" No, he did not identify himself, just asked to speak to me. Daddy tells him I'm not home. Still no ID. So, Daddy begins asking, "Is this Dan? Is this Kevin? Is this Jerry?" Including all the boyfriends whose names he knew. Finally, I guess Jack got the message and did say who he was and that he would call back later. Mama heard it all.

I never knew what she said to Daddy because by the time I got home, he was hiding behind the newspaper in the living room. She met me at the door and told me the whole thing. Lord, this was like a tale of dumb and dumber. "Don't wait for him to call. You call him back right now." So, I did. It wasn't exactly a private conversation. We only had one phone and it was on the wall in the kitchen, as it was at Jack's house. I called him back, with, I'm sure, both sets of parents eavesdropping. He asked me on a date, to a basketball game. I, of course, said yes.

The game was on Saturday night. Jack came to the door, was invited in to say hello, clearly scared to death, and I don't know why. Daddy had been his Sunday School teacher so he wasn't a stranger, nor was Mama. Maybe he was scared of me. When we got to the car, he clearly knew that he was supposed to open the door for me. But he didn't. He just stood there, so, after an awkward pause, I opened the door and got in, thinking he would at least close the door. Nope, again, he just stood there. On our next date, he at least opened the car door, just didn't close it. But the third date was the charm. He finally got it and both opened and closed the car door.

That first date was a little iffy, too. Jack played in the band, which played at all the basketball games so we had to sit close to the band. Every time they played, he had to get up and join them. They played before the game, at the end of each quarter and after the game. So, it was a back-and-forth date. I would have appreciated his undivided attention, but the trumpet player had another obligation. Our second date echoed the first, but at least this time, I knew what to expect. On our third date, we went to the movies, a much more ordinary date. After, we went to the Dairy Queen, along with everybody else in Paducah on a date that night. We each ordered a coke and got an order of French fries to split. That was pretty much how we ended each date until we started parking and necking before he took me home.

After the basketball games, I decided that I liked Jack and wanted to see more of him. It so happened that we were assigned the same seat in study hall in the library, only I was there third period and he came for the fourth period. I always lingered at the table until I saw him coming, then grabbed my books and met him coming as I was going. Always smiled and said, "Hi, Jack," to which I got a nod and a mumbled "Hi." That was it. Better than nothing. We dated, but didn't go steady. I dated other boys at school until someone else came into my life.

Our neighbors, the Leslies, were a nice young couple with one little girl. She was a stay-at-home mom and he worked in some office downtown, maybe an insurance company. I always remember his five white dress shirts hanging on the clothesline every week. Admired her for all the ironing that entailed.

Well, they had another baby, a boy this time. That meant that their house was now too small. They needed a third bedroom so they bought a larger house, but their house didn't go on the market. They sold it to the senior Leslies, Curtis and Hattie. Their house was too big because all but one of their three kids were married. Only the youngest remained and he was off at college.

I don't remember what Mr. Leslie did for a living. Mrs. Leslie was a first-grade teacher. Our new neighbors were quite a pair. Combative, I believe, describes them best. Their bathroom window was opposite our bedroom windows. Every morning, they fought. Yelled at each other at the top of their voices. We could even tell when he left the bathroom and she took over the room.

But that was not all. On occasion, if he tried to leave, she would block his way by standing behind the car in the driveway so he couldn't back out. Of course, they were yelling at each other. I think she was lucky he never ran over her, even though he would rev the engine like he was going to.

Once, I saw him get revenge. She had spent most of Saturday planting flowers and trimming bushes in their yard. The next day, yes, Sunday, he pulled up every flower, cut the bushes to the ground, and threw them all in the driveway. We would not have been surprised if one had murdered the other. And that was not the only time he would have been a candidate for murder.

One day I came home from school and could tell something was wrong. Mama was fit to be tied. Turns out, Mr. Leslie had come for a visit, and had, hum. how can I put this nicely? There is no way to put it nicely, fondled her breasts. She slapped him and kicked him out of the house. He never darkened our door again.

But the Leslies did have a plus, at least so I thought, their youngest son, Clint. I think he ran out of tuition money, so he came home to live with them. He pursued me, and I fell for him, hook, line, and sinker. My parents didn't say anything, but I know they were watching. He was older, more sophisticated. Jack didn't measure up, and was put on the back burner. I was in pretty much over my head, but did not realize it. Clint pushed the sex thing really hard, to the point that sometimes I was scared. He always honored my "No," but I was not sure he always would. Birth control was mostly left up to the boy who sometimes didn't get the seriousness of unwed pregnancy. In those days, getting pregnant out of wedlock was a shame to the girl and her family. Girls were sent away to have the baby in secret. I had no intention of letting that happen. I had plans, and they did not include having a baby when I was an unwed teenager.

Clint joined the Army. Thanks, Daddy! He did his basic training at Fort Knox. When it was time for him to graduate, he wanted me to come with his parents to the graduation ceremony and parade. Mama and Daddy said I could go, so I went.

Oh, my word! There has never in the history of the world been a worse trip! Either the Leslie's car didn't have a back seat or it was full of luggage because I had to sit in the front seat between them. It was crowded, to say the least. You can only pretend to be asleep so much. I had to bite my tongue to keep from saying over and over again," Are we there yet?"

Then we finally were there. At Fort Knox, there is a roundabout. Mr. Leslie, who probably had never seen one, couldn't figure it out. We went round and round, with Mrs. Leslie yelling at him the whole time, and he yelling back. Finally, he figured out where to get off. We stayed in a motel that night. I had to share the room with them. Ugh! We couldn't see Clint because all the grads were confined to quarters until the next morning. We only got to see him after the ceremony and parade were over. Then all we could do was go to lunch with him. For this I had to ride umpty jillion miles with those people? And we still had to go home.

In a few days Clint came to Paducah on leave before he had to report to his first assignment. I broke up with him. He didn't take it well. What clinched the deal was his behavior when we went to a ball game. There was a big crowd pushing to get in, and he was squeezing the rear ends of some of the ladies, then denying it when they turned around and accused him. He thought it was funny. I thought the apple didn't fall far from the tree. By the way, my parents were elated.

With Clint gone, Jack moved to the front burner again. Senior year started up, and so did we. As soon as we got our class rings, Jack asked me to go steady and I told him yes. Going steady meant that I wore his class ring. Since it was too big, I wrapped tape around it until it fit. Not very pretty, but there was no other way.

Going steady with Jack meant that I entered the world of ham radio. He got his license at sixteen, he and his best friend, Don Miller. His ham shack was set up in his bedroom, which was up in the converted attic in their house. His sister Susan's room was across the stair landing which was why I was allowed to go up there.

Jack lived and breathed ham radio. He was on the air every chance he got. He and Don would play tennis, then went home and talked to each other on the radio. I never got that. The neighbors were not overly happy with the ham next door. The reason was that his radio signal interfered with their TV reception. They could hear his voice, and not the voices on TV. In ham radio, the way you indicate that you want to connect with another ham is by saying, "CQ, CQ, CQ," until someone comes back to you. The neighbors' little grandson was learning the alphabet, only he would say, "A, B, C, Q, C, Q." Jack finally got some device that blocked his signal, and all was well.

The Prom was coming up, and Jack couldn't dance. His mother tried to teach him and he did get to where he could shuffle around the floor, but he hated it. More than ballroom dancing, he hated rock and roll, and the Twist. It just was not his thing and he never willingly did it. But he tried for my sake. We went to the Prom, and I, at least, had a good time.

Now, we had a dog, a Pekinese named Toy Ling, with a big, fluffy tail. I don't remember much about him. Probably because he was a dog and not a cat.

I also don't know whose idea it was to get a dog in the first place, but he showed up sometime during Daddy's thirty-day leave after he returned from Greenland. One afternoon, Daddy was backing the car out of the driveway and hit him. Toy Ling let out a yowl and we all came running. As I recall, my Aunt Anne and Uncle Charlie were there. Just as I burst out of the back door, I saw Daddy running toward him with a raised hammer in his hand. Toy Ling was yowling and flopping around, so Daddy was going to put him out of his misery.

I intervened. It wasn't as bad as it sounded, but it was bad. His right eye was hanging out of the socket. After that, I don't remember exactly what took place, but I was now in the house in hysterics. To get me under control, Mama slapped me. I slapped her back! Still not under control, I threw an ashtray. It hit the low, round Japanese lacquerware table and chipped off a piece on top. That was always a reminder of that awful day. Wherever Daddy was going when he hit the dog, he left Mama and me to deal with the situation. Mama called the vet and then a taxi to take the dog and me to his clinic. She couldn't go with me because we had company. The vet was able to put the eye back in its socket, but the sight was gone. Thereafter, the eye was also just a bulging, cloudy reminder of the day I slapped my mama. Anyway, he recovered. Even though he wasn't a cat, I loved him. He was my buddy.

We moved to Ft. Eustis, and then to Paducah. More tragedy was on the way. Toy Ling roamed the neighborhood. There were no leash laws, and no one had a fence. I think he visited most of the neighbors almost every day.

This time, he was crossing the street and a car hit him on his blind side. I heard the yelp and the thud, and ran out. Toy Ling was lying dead in the street and the car was driving off. The driver didn't stop. I stood in the middle of the street yelling, "Come back here! You killed my dog!" The driver turned right at the corner and was gone. So was Toy Ling. Daddy buried him in the backyard.

Senior year rolled on and graduation and college loomed in our future. We were going separate ways, Jack to UK and I to Lambuth. We agreed that we couldn't keep up a long-distance relationship so when it was time, I gave his ring back. We were still friends but didn't want to be tied down when there was so much ahead. Obviously, that was not the end.

We were active at church. Mama belonged to a Bible Study circle and volunteered as a teacher for Vacation Bible School. One time she was going to do a program for circle that I guess involved our time in Japan because she was going to wear her kimono. She needed me to help her put on the obi. The obi is the wide decorative "belt" that holds the kimono together. Hers was pre-tied, otherwise, she would have had to tie it herself, and it is beyond complicated. In back, it's a big, flat bow. Nevertheless, she was going to need my help. You just can't do it by yourself. It wraps around the body, there are tucks that must happen, then it is secured around the waist with an ornate band that is tied in front. I would have to be late for school because the circle didn't meet until 9:30. She wrote me a late excuse. I don't think it said that I had to help my

Mama get dressed. Later, she did tell me that the ladies were fascinated with the kimono and obi.

Mama and I did something else together. This was fun. It was Halloween. We had had a steady stream of Trick or Treaters come to the door. It was getting late; the kids had just about quit coming. In the lull, Mama suddenly had the idea that we should go trick or treating next door. These were young neighbors with two little kids, certainly NOT the Leslies. We put on overcoats and masks and knocked on their door. When our neighbor saw us, she was not pleased. "You all are awful big to be out trick or treating, don't you think?" she said as she dropped candy in our bag, one tiny piece each. "You should be ashamed of yourselves," and shut the door in our faces. We almost burst, holding in our laughter until we got back to our house. She never knew it was us.

Also, at church, Daddy became the Baptist Tabernacle Treasurer. That meant that not only did he keep the books, but he counted the money from the offering every Sunday. After Sunday dinner, he dumped the offering on the kitchen table and we counted it. I usually counted the cash and change, mostly from Sunday School. It had to be counted twice to be sure it was accurate. I also learned how to fill out a deposit slip. On Monday, Daddy dropped off the checks and cash at church so the Secretary could record the donations. I was sworn to absolute secrecy about what I knew about who gave what and how much.

And I helped Mama, too. On Saturday, I had to clean the bathroom. Not my favorite job, especially since I usually had to do it over, because the first time was rarely good enough. I had to re-clean the bathtub and this time, use the Comet. Wipe the bottom of the commode, wipe around the doorknob, etc., etc. I hate to clean bathrooms.

Something I hated more than cleaning the bathroom was helping with the laundry. Initially, we had only a wringer washer. Clothes were dried on the clothesline in the back yard. That meant we ran the clean clothes through the wringer on the machine into a basket to take to the clothesline. The clothesline had to be wiped off-very well-so any dirt on the line would not transfer to where the clean clothes were pinned to the line. Then the clothes were hung to dry. Then, of course, they had to be taken down, either folded or put aside for ironing later. I still had to iron the pillowcases and Daddy's handkerchiefs. Thankfully, his uniforms were taken to the cleaners for professional laundering and ironing.

We finally got a real washer and dryer. That meant the old washing machine moved out of the kitchen nook and a table and chairs moved in. The new washer and dryer were installed in the kitchen. We lost some lower cabinets and some space, but it was still much better.

Something else the moved into the nook was a coo-coo clock. I don't know where it came from. I suspect it was a gift from someone because I don't think it would have been Mama's choice. Just like a grandfather clock, you get used to the chiming. You hear it, but it just does not really register in your consciousness. But sometimes we did hear, actually, not hear, the coo-coo clock. It got cold back in the nook during the winter months. Coo-coo didn't like the cold weather. When the hour came, the two little people on either side of the coo-coo house spun slowly instead of fast, and coo-coo came out and said, "Coo." That was it. He was cold and had no more to say. We always listened to see if he would finish his song.

You've got to learn things out of school as well as in. Two things I learned in Paducah: how to water ski and how to drive a stick shift car.

Jack's dad had a boat. When Jack learned that I didn't know how to waterski, he took it upon himself to teach me. We went to the river, the Ohio River. Don usually came along, sometimes Susan. Papa Green drove the boat. Very rarely did Jack get the boat by himself. His daddy wanted control.

As I think of that big river now, I wonder why anyone would allow their child to even be on it, much less to waterski. There are huge barges with big wakes going up and down, plus, the river is swift. The Ohio is not a lazy river. It is dangerous.

There was a substantial sandbar upriver, on the Illinois side, where we could beach the boat. This was where we got ready to ski. Jack showed me how to put the skis on, and told me how to stand up once the boat got going fast enough to keep you upright. He kept his eyes on me while his daddy drove. After a few clumsy falls, I got it. I could ski!

Skying along behind the boat was OK, but there was something else that was more fun. That was skying outside the boat's wake. It took a little doing, but once you were outside the wake, you could really fly. If you leaned way over, you could almost catch up to the boat. Then, you could also go back and forth, across the wake on both sides. So much fun. On occasion, we would follow the barges and ride their wake, but only after Papa Green let Jack take the boat without him. Doing that was not the best idea. Then there were the times when two people skied in tandem. If you stayed out of each other's way, you were alright.

One time my daddy went with us to learn how to ski. Try as he could, he just could not get up. I guess the old football player's legs were not up to the challenge anymore. But I did give him an A for effort.

Now, learning to drive a stick shift. It's not like I had a car. It would be years before I had a car of my own. But my girlfriend from my Girl Scout troop had a VW with a stick shift. She thought I ought to learn to drive her car. So, we sat out on a mission. We went to the parking lot of the Lutheran church down the street. The parking lot was empty so there was no danger of my running into anything.

I got behind the wheel. Gloria told me how and when to shift, had me move the stick a few times, push the pedals, and I started the car. The initial results were not good. I bucked that little car all over that parking lot. We laughed until we cried. Clearly, this was not going to come easy.

Finally, she gave up, at least for then. We went back two more times before I finally mastered that stick shift. There were a few times when that skill came in handy. Bet I couldn't do it today.

My time In Paducah came to an unofficial end when I left for college. Of course, Mama and Daddy still lived there and I still called it home. And, Jack was there, and his parents, too. Some of those last two years of high school were good, some not. But that could have been the same anywhere. Paducah was home because my parents were there, not because I felt a real connection to the place itself. That was as it always was. Home was my parents.

And I do have a special place in my heart for Paducah because my parents are still there.

Made in the USA
Columbia, SC
31 March 2023

14334609R00131